Teaching with
EQUITY

Strategies and Resources for Building a Culturally Responsive and Race-Conscious Classroom

Aja Hannah

Published by:
ULYSSES PRESS
PO Box 3440
Berkeley, CA 94703
www.ulyssespress.com

ISBN: 978-1-64604-356-9
Library of Congress Control Number: 2022932318

Printed in the United States by Kingery Printing Company
10 9 8 7 6 5 4 3 2 1

Acquisitions editor: Claire Sielaff
Managing editor: Claire Chun
Project editor: Renee Rutledge
Editor: Lauren Schiffman
Proofreader: Joyce Wu
Front cover design: Ashley Prine
Cover artwork: from shutterstock.com—students © Batshevs; books ©
    Marina Akinina
Interior design: what!design @ whatweb.com
Production: Winnie Liu

CONTENTS

INTRODUCTION

Why do we need equity when we have equality? Weren't Black kids bussed to White schools? Didn't we strike down "separate but equal" in the 1950s?

Yes. We did. We also created a culture of assimilation instead of integration. We ignored the beautiful differences in our communities and country. We ignored the disadvantages and hurdles placed in front of certain groups of people.

Equality is when every student is given the same resources in order to succeed. This sounds good until equality isn't enough to make up for the deficits history or public policy has created.

That's where equity steps in. **Equity** is when you give specialized tools to certain students so that all kids are on a level playing field. A synonym for "equity" is "fairness."

What is Equality? These definitions may be hard to understand, so imagine you have a classroom of students all learning to read. You give five minutes of individual instruction to every student after a lesson. Some students don't need the five minutes. They already understood the lesson. Some students use the five minutes, and the subject matter clicks. Then there is one student that needs more than five minutes. They are almost there. They just need something more. So you or an aide gives the student some more time. That's an example of surpassing equality and finding equity.

What is Equity? Here's another example. Imagine a wall in front of a blackboard. The wall cannot be removed. Three students are standing in front of the wall, trying to see over it. One student is tall enough to see over it, and he dutifully takes notes. The other two are shorter to different degrees. They cannot see over the wall to the blackboard. A way to make this situation equal is to give everyone—even the tallest child—a stepping stool to see over the wall. But what if this stepping stool is still too short for the shortest child? Is it OK because everything is equal? Is it OK because the two tallest children say they can see fine?

A way to make the blackboard situation equitable is to give the two shorter children stools that make them the same height as the tallest child; that may mean having different-sized stools and that the tallest child doesn't get a stool. Now everyone can see over the wall at the same height. That is what this book hopes to do for the classroom.

When I was a first-year student in high school, I took a test in math class that included a word problem about a baseball game. The word problem assumed I knew how many innings were in a baseball game. It assumed I knew the mechanics of a game. I did not. I could not figure out the answer without this information, and it turned out that many of the other students in the class could not either.

After the teacher graded the questions, we asked him why he didn't provide this information. He said it was "common knowledge." The class erupted with shouts of no and even some students remarking that it wasn't fair. We weren't aware we needed to know about baseball. What did baseball have to do with math?

The teacher asked how many of us got it wrong, and over half the students raised their hands. He decided not to count the question as part of our grades but to let those who got it right earn extra credit. Then he half-heartedly reprimanded us for not knowing something so common.

This. This right here is why equity is needed in classrooms. This teacher had been using the same question for years without looking at it in relation to the diversity in his class. His advanced math class had changed from primarily cisgender White men like himself to a mixture of White and brown and Asian girls and boys, many of whom did not care about America's favorite pastime.

This teacher's "common knowledge" question became a challenge for students who were different. While his test question was dealt out equally to each student, it was not equitable.

How often does this happen without teachers realizing it? How can teachers who want to do better, do better?

As a disclaimer, this book is not focused on critical race theory and is not a guide on how to talk about race with your students. This book also does not cover equity in relation to other aspects of life like neurodivergence or LGBTQ (lesbian, gay, bisexual, transgender, and queer) issues. These talks are long and complex, and although they intersect with racial equity, there is not enough space in this book to give these areas any comprehensive justice.

Teaching with Equity focuses on racial equity for Black, Asian, and Latinx Americans as well as the Indigenous people of the US, including Native Hawaiians. Anti-racist activists may think I'm going easy on Racism with a capital R, and it is true that I'm going to try to avoid this word and some of the harder parts of racism.

I'm doing this because I want to see change in classrooms, even if it is the littlest change. I want all teachers to be receptive to the suggestions in this book. Sometimes the word racism or racist can be triggering to the White community. This book may be assigned or suggested reading for teachers who are not necessarily on board with changing how things have always been done. I don't want them to get hung up on their feelings and miss the larger picture.

I also want to make issues of race easy to understand. While racism is a complex and intersecting issue in education and no one race is a monolith, there are some common difficulties that can be addressed. Because no one person can speak for their race or all races, I have interviewed some experts who have shared personal history, community stories, and expert knowledge.

Common threads of racism for people of color include colorism, sexualization and fetishization, microaggressions, and marginalization when it comes to representation in the US. Children of color are aware of these issues even in elementary school. Then there are topics specific to each race or culture like slavery for Black students or the model minority myth for East Asian students.

Kids discuss these topics with their parents and grandparents behind closed doors, and even the youngest of students feel issues of racism. It is important to address these differences and to teach with equity at the start of a child's educational career.

Why Elementary School? They Are So Young

Why not elementary school? Why not start at the foundation and build a child up? When you build a castle, you start at the bottom and give it a sturdy, secure base. When your child is young, you introduce healthy foods first like mushed carrots or squash. As they get older, they may not like vegetables or fruits, but you still offer those foods because you want to build a healthy, well-rounded kid. You don't suddenly introduce vegetables in high school when their palate is already developed.

Why would you wait until children are in middle or high school to address racial inequity that the students can so clearly see with their own eyes?

Elementary school students of color are already familiar with issues of race and inequity. They hear their grandparents and parents talk among themselves. They are given lessons on how their race may impact their lives and how they need to conduct themselves to stay safe or not be seen as a target.

If children of color are mature enough to handle these conversations, so are White children.

A Lack of Time/Money/ Support/Knowledge

As a former educator and a mom of two, I know that teachers do not have extra time, so I have made sure that most of the materials I reference can be found as audiobooks or videos online. This way, you can listen to information in the background as you set up your classroom, grade tests, drive to work, or wash the dishes.

Ernest J. Wilson III is a professor of communication and political science at the University of Southern California's Annenberg School for Communication and Journalism. In an interview with me, he spoke about how his son Rodney teaches secondary school and has so many forms to fill out. Wilson is happy that, as a professor, he doesn't have all that paperwork or lesson planning.

Wilson understands that change, especially uncomfortable change, is difficult to do. "We have to give people the human recognition that this is hard. We have to learn to be comfortable with being uncomfortable. That's easy to say until it's eight in the morning and you have to drop your kids off at school or your refrigerator goes out," he said.

What I think he means is that it's easy to think you will be intentional and do your best and try to make the world a better place. You may have plans to learn about the wars and oppressions. But then life—daily life—hits you, and you don't have time to read or listen to a whole podcast.

I know that you are limited in your resources, in your budget, in what you are even allowed to teach. I have tried to accommodate these things so that you do not need to stretch yourself any thinner.

There are no cookie-cutter answers, but there are some easy ways to lead the change, for example, by using the tables of names in Chapter 10 when you create word problems. Instead of using the name Brian or the default Anglo-Saxon name when creating class materials, try Bao or Booker or Bontu.

SECTION I

THE BIG PICTURE

I have been in elementary classrooms throughout the country and they all have similarities. No matter whether the school has a library or not, the classroom has its own set of books. Sometimes these are just old, donated textbooks. Other times, a teacher's private collection of fiction and nonfiction takes up a whole wall or two. At the beginning of a school year, the walls are usually more bare, waiting for student art work and collaborative classwork. Some teachers front-end the year with projects and class rules so they have something to hang. Other teachers buy materials from party supply or education stores to start. Still other teachers evenly space out the time it takes to fill their walls.

The thing is—no matter the kind of teacher you are—you are a teacher. This big picture is a starting point, whether you're a first-year or a seasoned pro. Tack the chance to evaluate yourself in a way you probably have not before.

Similarly, every student is a student, and underrepresented students face challenges that are closely related. You may recognize one or two of these barriers to equity from the news or a study that you read—like the school to prison pipeline—and how these challenges connect to a particular type of student. However, depending on the demographic of the area, the barrier to equity can actually be applied to under-represented students across all races throughout the country. It's best to know these common, big picture topics well so that you have a starting point no matter where you teach, now or in the future.

Chapter 1

ESTABLISH A BASELINE

We are hitting the ground running. There are a lot of facts, and you don't have a lot of time. You're a teacher. Are you trying to read this on your 30-minute lunch break? That's a joke. There is no lunch break. Just planning periods and lunch duty.

How to Find Your Baseline

So let's jump into this thing called teaching with equity. This chapter breaks down establishing a baseline for your school, your classroom, your students, and yourself. Finding this baseline will help you identify your areas of opportunity—as the positivity heads like to call it—and take advantage of the tips on how to build comfort in your classroom so that the issue of race is not taboo. To find your baseline, start with your classroom.

The Classroom:

- Are there photos of children and their families?
- Are there photos of children from around the world in traditional clothing?
- Are there photos of children from around the world in Western clothing?
- How integrated is the student seating?

The People—Take stock of your school, your classroom, and your students:

- What is the racial makeup of the students at your school?
- What is the racial makeup of the students in your classroom?
- What is the racial makeup of the teachers at your school?
- Compare this to the racial makeup of the US today.
- Compare this to the racial makeup of projections for the US in 10 years, i.e. when your students may be in the "real world."

The Books—Look at the literature in your classroom and its representation:

- How many books were written by people of color?
- How many books were written by women?
- Do the authors of these books represent all facets of the US?
- Is there more than one story from each race represented by the kids in the classroom?
- Are BIPOC (Black, Indigenous, people of color) stories limited to explaining cultural traditions like stone soup?

The Technology:

- What kind of communication technology is available to your students?
  - » Zoom?
  - » FaceTime?
  - » Chat groups?
- What programs are used during education, and what is the default avatar?

- How can a student change their avatar to be more representative?

- What videos do children watch? How diverse are the characters?

  » Are the BIPOC characters developed or stereotypes?

The Curriculum:

- How are Indigenous people described in the history of the US, if at all?

- How often are BIPOC credited with discoveries and inventions outside of their month (Black History Month, etc.)?

- How often are BIPOC empowered and included in curriculum when their race is not the focus of the text?

Now that you've asked yourself these questions and established the baseline you're currently working with, do the following exercises to evaluate your baseline. Where can you make your classroom more equitable?

Exercise One: Look at your classroom with fresh eyes. How or where would BIPOC students see themselves represented in your classroom? Do this for every race.

Exercise Two: Look again. How would non-Latinx students perceive a Latinx person? Would they even see that person at all? Do this for every race.

The Breakdown

Where do students of color see themselves represented? Where do White students learn about people of other races? Is it just in the pictures of people of other races as slaves or servants, with maybe an occasional inventor included? Do students of color see stereotypes of themselves in the photos on the wall, or do they see portraits of successful Americans that happen to look like them?

How do your White students learn about students of other races? Do they see a student in Africa in a grass skirt sitting under a Baoban tree with a single male instructor or could they look like just another American in a crowd?

Too often, people of color and children of color are depicted in stereotypical ways. They are caricatures of their culture in traditional clothing in portraits, or they appear in books that teach about a historical or cultural holiday. While cultures and history are important to talk about, the rest of the person gets marginalized and pigeonholed.

Even in technology and TV programming, minority groups are underrepresented. For example, in many Disney films, if a main character is a minority, they end up turning into something. In *The Princess and the Frog*, Princess Tiana turns into a frog for most of the movie. In *Soul*, Joe Gardner turns into a ghost-like apparition and then a cat. Kuzco turns into a llama in *The Emperor's New Groove,* and Kenai from *Brother Bear* turns into a bear. *In Turning Red,* Mei Lee turns into a red panda. Of the 13 minority main characters in Disney films to date, five turn into animals, whereas only one of the 23 White main characters in Disney films turns into an animal. Maybe two if you count the Beast from *Beauty and the Beast.* Representation of minority races as main characters is already slim, and then studios further erase the visual representation.

In the popular television show *Daniel Tiger's Neighborhood,* most of the characters are animals except for the human Prince Wednesday and his family, who are White royalty, and the human Miss Elaina and her family, who are Black. Miss Elaina refers to everyone as "toots," just like her mother apparently. In 2018, the show added the Platypus family, who are clearly

Chinese under all their platypus fur. The mother wears a jade necklace, and the grandmother wears traditional Chinese clothing. While *Daniel Tiger's Neighborhood* is a great show for social and emotional development, race representation is not its strong suit.

Start Where You Are

You have no power to change certain things about your school, like the number of BIPOC teachers, the diversity among your students, and the media the students consume on their own time. And you cannot currently make certain changes to your classroom, like buying a ton of new, diverse literature. I get that.

Teaching with Equity is not asking you to do more on your (already) shoestring budget. It's about taking advantage of what you have at your disposal, utilizing free resources, and working within your abilities to expand your students' views.

Your baseline can help identify areas where you may come up short, and generate ideas for improvements. Some things are easier to fix than others. Look at what you can change in your classroom. Add or switch out posters and photos. Empower students to change their avatars. Change up the literature. Supplement historical educational materials. Use modified worksheets for inclusivity. Get involved with a modern version of pen pals, so students can visually communicate with kids their age across the globe.

For diverse books and classroom resources—including some for free—refer to Chapter 10.

Learn about Yourself

Taking a closer look at yourself can show you where your opportunities for change lie. Find your weaknesses, and learn about what implicit biases you may have. "Implicit biases" are attitudes or beliefs you hold about certain people or groups without realizing it. These biases do not come from conscious thoughts, but they do show themselves in actions. An example of implicit bias in action follows.

> Jamal, a kindergarten student, is being loud and disruptive again. He won't stop running in the hallway, and he shouts out his answers. Every time this happens, the teacher puts him in time out right away. When that does not work, the teacher tells his mother about his behavior when she comes to pick him up at the end of the day.

> Meanwhile, Kyle is also a rambunctious kindergartener. He speaks out of turn and can't stop himself from running to recess. He's just so excited. His teacher attributes this to his young age and "boys being boys." His teacher warns him several times to use his indoor voice and wait his turn. Kyle tries, but he doesn't always listen. At the end of the day, Kyle does receive one time out. Since it is only one time out, the teacher does not tell his mother.

These two kids have essentially the same issues, but notice my word choices in describing these two boys. For Jamal, I chose "disruptive," and for Kyle, I chose "rambunctious." This sets the tone for how the teacher and the reader view each student. These internal word choices are a reflection of the implicit biases that Jamal's and Kyle's teacher has when she thinks of her students. She's not doing this on purpose. She may not even realize there is a difference, but I'll tell you now that Jamal sees it.

Despite having the same problems, Jamal is disciplined every time and swiftly. Kyle is approached more thoughtfully. The only difference between them is their race. One has a typically Black name, and the other has an Anglo-Saxon name.

This example plays out in real life time after time in classrooms across the US. I will speak more about this specific issue in Chapter 2, but implicit biases like this need to be stopped and challenged.

The only way to know your biases is to suss them out, and it is an uncomfortable reflection. Harvard University's Project Implicit has designed Implicit Association Tests that, according to its website, measure "attitudes and beliefs that people may be unwilling or unable to report." You can find this test at implicit. harvard.edu.

After completing the test or tests, you receive the results with interpretations. The interpretations are based on research done by scholars at the University of Washington, the University of Virginia, Harvard University, and Yale University. The tests include one based on race along the Black and White split, but tests also focus on the Asian American and White split, on Arab or Muslim versus others split, a light skin versus dark skin split, and so on.

I challenge you to take the tests.

Listen, it's going to be yucky feeling, but it's OK. It's about becoming a better you for your students. When you get your results, you may feel the push to ignore or minimize them. Don't. Instead, focus on how you can identify and unlearn the implicit biases you have.

Fun Fact

If you haven't guessed by now, I am a Black woman, and I write about anti-racism, among a thousand other topics. Even I had a skewed bias toward White people when I first took the test. I was raised by a White woman in an upper-middle-class—*read White*—neighborhood in the suburbs. Most of my friends were White or Asian. I went to a White university and started teaching at primarily White schools.

To work on my bias, I have examined some of the judgments and stereotypes I have about my own people and about other races. I figured out where these thoughts came from, and when they enter my mind now, I challenge them. I have sought out others and listened to them speak on racism across communities, and I listen when I am told I've said something hurtful.

I wince at the insensitivity I used to show and how I embraced certain stereotypes when they fit my agenda or when they were positive. Just because a stereotype is positive, it doesn't mean it is right or OK. A positive stereotype can still be damaging.

I will talk about some common implicit biases and what the resulting microaggressions look like in Chapter 2.

Survey Your Students

If your students are old enough, give them a written survey to see what they think of race and racism.

You may want to keep it anonymous, as your goal is to build comfort in your classroom. You want students to be able to feel comfortable talking and learning about race. If they have a misconception about a certain racial group and they get pushback from other students, they may not ask their next question. They may, instead, sit with their misconceptions and ignorance as they grow into young people and then adults.

If your students aren't old enough to answer a written survey, you can ask students their thoughts individually during or after all those assessments you have to do. Taking each student aside allows for privacy and honesty, especially for children who are shy or otherwise marginalized. Another idea is to send the survey home to parents. Perhaps a child will feel more comfortable answering these questions when their parents ask them, or maybe the child has confided in their parents about how they feel in the classroom.

Do not ask or expect answers from children of color when they are in front of their peers. They may feel pressured to fit in and modify their answers. I will talk more about assimilation versus integration in Chapter 2. Here is a sample survey for third, fourth, and fifth graders:

1. What is race?

2. What is racism?

3. Yes or no: I have heard people being teased at school about their race.

4. Yes or no: I feel like I belong in this class.

5. Yes or no: I have learned about other races and cultures in school.

6. Circle the answer(s): I identify as Black, White, Asian, Latino, Pacific Islander, Indigenous person or Native American, or multiracial.

When you get your results, it is important not to take the average or the majority as fact. If your class is majority White, the students may not have seen or heard someone being teased about their race at school. They may feel like, of course, they belong.

If possible, pay attention to the trends that you see in the minority students. What have they seen or heard? How do they feel they are represented in the school?

Build Comfort in the Classroom

Now that you have surveyed your class, you can recognize what your students need from you and from one another to create an equitable classroom. Building comfort is about teaching students how to ask questions and giving them the space to feel they can ask tough questions. Integrating and practicing the steps below are a good way to start creating that comfortable space in your classroom.

Step 1: School is about learning, and it starts from the top down. Even if you are a person of color, reach beyond what you know and learn about another race so you can educate your students. Model this behavior by admitting when you don't know things. Show students how to reach out to find answers.

Step 2: Be open about discussions of race as long as they aren't hurtful. If certain topics seem triggering or exhausting to students of color, let them opt out. You'll have to be their advocate. Refer to Step One. Remember: Students of color probably experience their own form of racism or hear accounts of racism from their community far more often than you do.

Step 3: Decide on the approach. Some classrooms have roundtable discussions with written rules and a set day or time. Some classrooms have free-form discussions as topics arise. Some have students put their questions in a box to be pulled out and answered anonymously. Some have a combination.

Step 4: Use the "call in" method. When a student says something hurtful, it is important to speak with that student. They may not know it is hurtful. They may be repeating something their parents or relatives or another adult said. They may not know where their hurtful belief comes from. An anti-racist educator, Liz Kleinrock, gave a 12-minute TED talk called "How to Teach Kids to Talk about Taboo Topics," in which she spoke on how she handled a student who said that White people may not have liked Black people because their skin was the color of poop. She used a "call-in" method rather than "calling out" the student in the classroom so that everyone could learn without discrimination or discouragement. This type of discussion does not need to be in private but it does need to be sensitive to both sides. The focus should not be on the students who were wronged or the student who said something hurtful. It should focus on the content and context of the statement. I give more details about how to use this method in your classroom in the "What to Do When You Hear a Colorist Conversation in the Classroom" section "What to Do When You Hear a Colorist Conversation in the Classroom" on page 38.

Kleinrock spoke more about her method in an interview for the Learning Together feature "Addressing Anti-Asian Racism with Students" on the Smithsonian Asian Pacific American Center website. She also has a website called Teach and Transform where she has resources and lesson plans for anti-racist teaching, including work-sheets on social justice.

Talking about racism isn't easy. I remember when I was in my first year as a substitute teacher in an elementary music classroom a few days before Martin Luther King Jr. Day (MLK Day). I was supposed to have the students sing a song about Martin Luther King Jr., so I asked the class if they knew who he was. The class stayed silent.

This was the middle of the day on a Friday. Surely, someone had talked with these students about why they had Monday off. So I tried to jog their memory and talked about how he gave the "I Have a Dream" speech and led a movement so people of all races could be equal. The students started to murmur among themselves and then asked what I meant by "equal." I explained how a while ago, people with different skin colors were treated differently. I gave the example that kids with different skin colors weren't allowed to go to school together. I told them that my own dad had to be bussed from his hometown to what was called a White school because it had better books and teachers. I explained how before Martin Luther King Jr. made his speeches, my dad wasn't allowed to go to that school.

One kid in the front—let's say Doug—asked if that meant he wouldn't be able to sit at the same table with his friend Jackson. I explained that if there hadn't been a fight for civil rights, Doug probably wouldn't have even met Jackson. Jackson wouldn't be allowed to go to school with him, and I wouldn't be allowed to be their teacher. Because of civil rights and Martin Luther King Jr., Doug and Jackson can be friends and sit at the same table and go to the same school. I asked, "Isn't that the good, important thing?"

There was a lot of chatter after this, and most of the kids demanded to know why. Why were people mean? Why weren't people allowed to be together? Why were people treated differently?

Once the room quieted down, I told the kids that there were many reasons this happened, but that didn't mean it was right or any of those reasons were good enough. I asked them to talk with their parents or their teacher more about this. Then we sang the song, and it was time for the kids to go back to their primary classroom.

I don't know why these students didn't know about Martin Luther King Jr. yet. I think it is easy for teachers to talk about MLK Day without realizing that students don't have the context of history. It's easier to say the good things than to say why the good things were necessary and that there were bad things before the good things. It is easier to say nothing than to try to figure out how to not hurt feelings or make someone uncomfortable. It is easier to say "ask your parents" than to have any angry parent or administrator in your classroom the next day.

I admit that when I realized I was running out of class time, I did default to the "ask your parents" tactic. Could I have handled it even better? Probably. As a first-year substitute, I was pretty green when it came to the hard topics and what could and could not be said in a classroom. But, even as a new teacher, I knew that teaching with equity meant addressing uncomfortable realities and histories in order for students to have all the pages of a story.

Teaching with equity helps students to comprehend who they are in the landscape today and to break down barriers to their own success. For students of color, it validates them; and for White students, it empowers them to help others. Doug and Jackson were good friends, and they sat closely for the rest of the class, talking to each other.

Reevaluate

After doing all this work, it is important to reevaluate your class. I would say to do it at least once during the school year, preferably after winter break. Take stock of your classroom, check in on your growth, talk to your students (who have no doubt grown as human beings), and find the areas you still need to work on.

According to the latest US Census, our country is becoming more diverse more quickly than anticipated. People of different races are falling in love and having children. The minority populations are continuing to grow while the White population is shrinking for the first time. From 2010 to 2020, growth of the White population fell by 8.6 percent in total. The largest group with growth was "two or more races" at 275.7 percent, followed by "other" at 46.1 percent, and then Asian at 35.5 percent. It should be noted that Latinx is not described as a race by the US Census, so many Latinx people classify themselves as "two or more" or "other," which is its own issue.

Even if your classroom, your city, or your state is still majority White, your students will need to know how to navigate a multiethnic world.

Chapter 2

COMMON CROSS-CULTURAL OPPORTUNITIES

So you've looked at your baseline and the areas in which you can improve. This chapter covers areas that offer common opportunities for improvement across racial backgrounds, such as assimilation versus integration, the police and prison pipeline, and common microaggressions. Microaggressions are subtle, indirect, and sometimes unintentional incidences of discrimination. Certain microaggressions are so common and so targeted that they have been nicknamed "dog whistles" because the significance of the discrimination is usually only caught by the target person of color.

An example of a dog whistle is using the word "ghetto" or "thug" to describe a young Black man who is causing trouble. These words are typically used only for Black men or men of color. When politicians reference "law and order," it is usually against protests from people of color or a reason to continue to enforce racially targeted policies like "stop and frisk." Other dog whistles include responding with "All lives matter" or "Blue lives matter" when someone refers to the Black Lives Matter protest.

Further, a dog whistle can be the response members of the media take when reporting an event. When reporting on a victim who is Black, journalists often relay that person's previous criminal history even if it is not relevant to the event. Meanwhile, when a White person commits a crime, their achievements are often listed alongside the crime they are accused of.

In this way, quiet racism fills in every spot of daily life. It can be disheartening for young students of color, especially when they can see the difference but do not have the words to express how unfair it is.

Fitting In, or Assimilation versus Integration

As mentioned briefly in the Introduction, the US desegregated schools in the 1950s and 1960s but never really integrated the schools. Assimilation is a process in which people become similar. In action, this means the minority groups assume the culture, values, and behaviors of a majority group. In the US, the majority is currently White people. Integration is the mixing of groups, through which the groups adopt cultures, values, and behaviors from one another. Assimilation is to equality what integration is to equity. Assimilation is a one-way street. Integration is a two-way street.

People of color assimilated into the White spaces in an effort not to stand out. This assimilation forcefully pushed down natural differences in culture and communities. For example, many Black women used chemical straighteners called relaxers so their hair looked like straight, White hair. Another example is the effort and pride of some bilingual or non-native English speakers to speak English without an accent.

Today, issues that students may have when assimilating are ignored, and students may not be forthcoming with their needs because they feel the pressure to act like the majority. Fitting in becomes more important than asking for help because asking for help means standing out, and the help is not always guaranteed.

Some common issues with assimilation that fall on the race equity line are socioeconomic gaps, European beauty standards, colorism, cultural appropriation, and the otherings of people of color.

How can you help your classroom integrate instead of assimilate? Try the following suggestions:

- Start by assigning ancestry research for homework. Have students ask their parents or relatives about their ancestry. Who's the oldest relative they know? How is that relative related to them? Where did that relative come from? Does anyone know how or when their ancestors came to the US? Students can bring in photos or stories or the oldest relative to share what they learned with the class. Note that students do not need to have all the answers. For many Black Americans, the ability to trace ancestry ends at their first freed ancestor. Other communities like Latino or Indigenous people have native roots in the Americas.

- Do an "I Am" poem assignment where the kids list the different things they are. Some versions of this include solid answers like "I am a sister. I am Black. I am a girl." Other versions get a little more creative. In *The Guide for White Women Who Teach Black Boys*, there is an "I Am" poem exercise that includes more personal answers, such as common greetings, items found in a student's home, or celebrated holidays.

- Celebrate holidays from many cultures. What is Yom Kippur? What is the Holi festival? What is Ramadan? Even if there are no students of these cultures or religions in class, learn about the reason for the holiday, what games may be played, and what food may be eaten. How does a first grader celebrate Juneteenth?

If you have the resources, have a small celebration in the classroom. If resources are sparse, pull up photos from around the world of these holiday celebrations and show them to students. Ask open-ended questions and encourage the students to ask questions. Then look up the answers together.

When it's a US holiday, talk about how it may or may not happen in other countries. What are the differences? What are the similarities? For many in Japan, a Christmas meal means fried chicken. Do people in Mexico celebrate Cinco de Mayo? (Some do but the bigger holidays are Day of the Dead and Carnival.)

- Recognize and value the racial differences inside and outside your classroom. In future chapters, I break down some of the challenges different races face in the classroom. Review these so you can recognize spaces for equity among your students.

Socioeconomic Issues

No race is limited to lower socioeconomic levels. Yes, there are wealthy people of every race across the globe. Yes, there are poor people of every race across the globe.

In the US, racist policies and structures have made—and still make—it difficult for people of color to break socioeconomic barriers. During slavery, Blacks were punished if they learned to read and write. After that, Jim Crow and "separate but equal" policies purposefully put Black people at a disadvantage when it came to education. Today, relics of redlining still affect the neighborhoods Black people live in and therefore the schools Black children go to.

For some Asian Americans, the struggle started around the time of the gold rush, when Chinese and South Asian immigrants were shipped in and used as laborers similar to indentured servants. After they finished building the railroads, they were scapegoated for everything from a rise in illnesses to small crimes and erased from history. Japanese immigrants and their descendants were pushed into Japanese internment camps during World War II. Other future Americans came as refugees to the US from Vietnam, Korea, and across South Asia after our wars destroyed their homes. (Over in Vietnam, they call it the American War.)

Did you know that the first Filipinos came to the Americas in the 1500s when the Spanish were trying to recruit Mexicans as soldiers? Many of these Filipinos never got to return home. The oldest permanent Filipino settlement in the US was founded in the 1700s in Louisiana.

In terms of Indigenous populations, thousands of people died from cold or hunger or disease on the Trail of Tears as they were forced to march from their homelands to reservations. Following that, the government continued to take their land—yes, even reservation land—and give it to White businesses and families. This practice continues today with the issues of the US government building pipelines on Indigenous land and the militarized response to protests. While these losses of land were costing native people resources and wealth, there was also a silent erasure of their culture. Child welfare workers took children from their homes and gave them to White people to be raised and educated and assimilated as US residents. Sometimes they were sent to the now-infamous boarding schools. The government banned cultural practices, songs, and dances.

Today, barriers to climbing the economic ladder affect all people of color, barriers that exist before a child is even in school. These include redlining, the breaking up of family units through drug abuse or the prison system, restrictive voter laws, and an unequal distribution of resources among public schools.

Despite pushes for equal opportunity employment, there are still issues of implicit biases during hiring or the uneven distribution of small-business loans. Many times, minority communities that did pull out of poverty saw their town burned to the ground, their people massacred, and the criminals left to walk free.

How Can Things Like Denial of a Small-Business Loan Affect Students?

When a minority is denied a small-business loan, that person must find another source of income or capital for their business or give up the idea of the project altogether. As an example, a Black woman cannot get funding to start her own business, so she has to work two jobs to support her family while she tries to save enough to start the business. Her husband, despite having a degree, was arrested for possession of marijuana a few years ago and now has a criminal record. Even though marijuana has become legal in their state, the husband is considered a criminal and has a tough time finding a job. No bank will lend him the money for a business.

The couple tries to petition their local government to change the law, but on voting day, the woman's job won't let her have time off to vote. She can't afford to be fired because the couple just had a child. Because they live in a low-income area, the school their child goes to is underfunded. Inexperienced first-year teachers enter the school ready to make a difference but burn out fast due to the lack of resources and administrative support.

In a few years, not much has changed. The woman has managed to save some money, but the money always seems to go to the car when it breaks down or unforeseen medical bills, like when their child broke an arm on the monkey bars. In school, the child struggles with math and the teacher doesn't have enough time to help. The child is bright but discouraged. The woman barely has time to make it to parent-teacher meetings let alone help the child with the new grid-style multiplication work that she struggles to understand. The woman's husband is now in jail for a parole violation because he took a ride with a friend to get to work, but that friend got pulled over for a failure to signal a lane change. Because the husband was on parole, the police searched the vehicle and found his friend to be in possession of drugs. The husband was also charged, and he wants to go to trial, but his public lawyer says he should take a plea deal that guarantees no jail time. The couple can't afford bail, so he sits in jail, trying to decide on doing a lengthy trial and missing more of his kid's life or taking a plea deal even though he is innocent.

This is an example of a poverty trap. Poverty traps keep people stuck in a cycle of poverty, purposefully making it difficult to build bridges out of the intentional and institutional poverty that many minorities find themselves in. It is built into our institutions in every aspect: education, childcare, health care, affordable housing, and more.

How Can You Help Students with Socioeconomic Stress?

You can't, not in a quick and easy way anyway. Fixing something as systemic as the socioeconomic disparities that minorities face takes education on the subject and then planning and lobbying to change policies. It is making sure votes can be cast for the right elected officials, and it requires marching in protests. It requires phone calls to local and state governments and writing letters to representatives. It requires more of you than you can probably give right now.

There are some things you can do in your classroom for students who face socioeconomic stress though. And the things you can do in class for these students add up:

- Make sure students have access to breakfast, lunch, and snacks they can take home.
- Allow children to fill their water bottles before they leave for home.
- Check that they are seeing the doctor, dentist, and optometrist regularly.
- Buy winter coats to use for recess or on the walk home.
- Have extra clean socks, underwear, and T-shirts.
- Spend extra time before or after school for tutoring or extracurricular activities.
- Allow time for homework, especially online work, to be done in class.
- Raise money for field trips.
- Go on field trips outside the neighborhood.
- Introduce successful people of color to the class.
- Have extra school supplies.
- Loan books, magazines, and other reading material.
- Direct parents to community resources, scholarships, grants, and job fairs.

Skin Color and European Beauty Standards

Kids are natural sharers, and when they are back from summer break, they like to compare tans. Sometimes this road can be bumpy to navigate. I don't know how many times in my childhood or even today that I have heard, "Wow, I'm almost as tan as you," or, "I'm darker than you!" Inevitably, someone pushes their arm against my arm to compare the colors.

My kids, who have just started preschool, have also started to get this comparison. We were hanging out at a pool one summer, and one of the regulars said, "Oh man. Your kids are already darker than me."

I said, "Yeah, they're part Black."

And she said, "Well, yeah, but I've been out in the sun every day, and I still can't get a tan like that."

And I said, "Yeah. Because they're Black."

Then the conversation ended. Was I too harsh? Maybe. But this conversation can be frustrating for people of color. How do I explain the dueling observation: White people want to get tanned like me, but then they still treat me as if I'm lesser? They want to have the same hair style but then they shake it off whenever it's not fashionable or whenever they need to speak to a manager. This skin color that they artificially delineated as "black" and placed so many stereotypes on is somehow OK for them to wear but not for me.

And let's not get started on using foods for skin tone like chocolate or honey or hazelnut. It's uncomfortable and makes people of color feel like an object. I have had people run their finger down my forearm as they tell me what flavor my skin color is, as if they are dipping their finger into a frosting jar and scooping a bit off the top. People of color are not commodities. They are people. Do not touch them out of curiosity. Do not let other students touch them out of curiosity. No one is entitled to any part of their body. There should be no unwanted stroking of their skin or hair or face.

This skin color topic leads to the larger issue of colorism, a form of stereotyping in which people judge others by the lightness or darkness of their skin. Colorism is similar to racism in that lighter skin colors are valued more highly than others. People of color who have lighter skin tend to find it easier to become employed, to become celebrities or models, and to be featured positively in visual media.

Notice the use of Photoshop. It's not just blemishes the media erases. Many times, the subject's skin color is lightened. Look at examples of Rihanna's *Vogue* magazine cover or Kerry Washington's *InStyle* cover. Magazines will claim it's "the lighting," but photographers and editors have admitted to touching up the photo.

This trend has led to the sale of Whitening or lightening creams all across the globe. From Bollywood to Latin America to Black America to Africa, people use these creams and sunscreens to stay as light as possible.

Because of this favoritism, light-skin and dark-skin people sometimes find themselves divided. In Black culture, people with lighter skin are sometimes called "high yellow" or "redbone." Lighter-skin students can be bullied, and some of the more "polite" terms include "Uncle Toms," "not Black enough," and "Oreos." On the flip side, dark-skinned students have been called "field hands," "purple black," and "midnight" to name a few.

In Asian culture, girls may be told to stay inside or protect their skin from the sun so they don't tan. Light skin can be seen as young, feminine, and upper class. Darker skin may be seen as dirty or aged by the sun. People with darker skin may be assumed to be lower class because they need to work in the sun. This is a particular stigma against South and Southeast Asians.

In Latino cultures, skin comes in all shades because the slave trade very much affected Central and South America. Color runs the gamut from Afro-Latino to White-passing Latino, but the darker skin can still be linked to lower socioeconomic communities. Simplified, Latino people who look White probably had ancestors from Spain, which conquered much of the region and held higher-ranking positions. Latino people who look darker tend to have ancestors who were native to the area or enslaved people who were brought to the area—both groups were usually lower-class citizens.

Across the ocean in Africa, examples of aggressive colorism still exist due to the lingering effects of apartheid. Before apartheid ended in South Africa in the 1990s, people were segregated by color in every manner, from schools to neighborhoods to what jobs they could hold. The darkest people were kept in the worst conditions and the White people were in the best conditions, but there was a special section for Colored or brown people that fit in between. Later, South Africa created a category for Indians separate from Colored.

Put simply, this kind of segregation gave people the false hope that they or their children could "work their way up" if they were light enough. Hence, the popularity of Whitening products. Segregation also created a class division among African people and sowed pervasive seeds of animosity in African communities. If the lower classes were busy being mean to one another, they wouldn't focus on the minority Whites who created the whole institution. Note that South Africa wasn't the only country under apartheid in Africa.

What to Do When You Hear a Colorist Conversation in the Classroom

In Chapter 1, I talked about "calling in" and how to gently have these conversations. If you are hearing something questionable in your classroom, come from a curiosity approach and ask your student questions. What did they say? What did they mean by it? Where have they heard this before?

Melanin Facts

- Melanin is nature's paint. It is what decides your pigment. Pigment determines the color of your hair, eyes, and skin.
- People with dark skin produce more melanin.
- More melanin means people with dark skin have more of a barrier against the sun's ultraviolet rays.
  - » People with darker skin get burned less than people with lighter skin.
  - » People with darker skin should still use sunscreen.
  - » People with darker skin can still get skin cancer.
- According to the latest research, more melanin could help protect skin against the effects of aging. See more at https://www.ncbi.nlm.nih.gov/pmc/articles/PMC7180973.

This conversation can be done as a class. Usually, there is very minimal privacy in a classroom and, if a student says something controversial, it is bound to be heard or spoken out later by the other children. Remember, this is supposed to be a learning experience rather than discipline. Privacy can make it seem secret or shameful.

After the student gives answers, follow up with why questions. Why does some skin tan more than other skin? Why is some skin darker than other skin? These questions can go to any student in the class. It is important that you do not put the pressure of answering these questions on the person of color.

If possible, bring knowledge into the conversation about the history of misconception. Explain how this topic could be uncomfortable or hurtful to others. Emphasize body positivity. It is important to do these last two parts. Yes, you want the student who innocently made the remark to be open to conversation, but you also want the person who was hurt by the comment to feel validated.

If one student needs to apologize to another, even if the remark was innocent, make sure it happens. Emphasize that apologies happen even when people make mistakes, but these mistakes can still hurt. Hurt can be real as if you stepped on someone's foot. Still an accident. Still painful.

What If the Impacted Peer Says They Want to Talk About It or It's OK?

If the peer wants to talk about it, they should feel empowered to do so. If you suspect it comes from a place of peer pressure, ask if that's what they really want. You can also later pull this student aside and come up with a code word. For example, the next time you ask the student if they are sure, they can say "It's OK" if everything is truly OK, or they can say "Yeah" if it's not OK. If they say "Yeah," then you know to shut down the behavior without peer pressure.

In elementary school, I would sit on the mat during circle time, and most times a student behind me would tug on my hair to see it spring. Many times teachers that saw this told the student to stop or keep their hands to themselves. Other times teachers would say that students could not touch my hair without permission. I would always give permission. In those days, I liked to show off how talented my hair was, and I was eager for friends. It was nice when teachers let me decide what to do with my body.

Explanations for Racism in Simple Sentences

"Some people in the US weren't treated fairly because of their skin color. Sometimes this still happens today, so our friends might be sensitive when you talk about the color of their skin."

"Did you know that people with brown skin and people with White skin were not allowed to go to school together? Your (great) grandparents may remember this. All because of their skin color. That doesn't seem fair, does it? So let's be mindful of the words we use to describe each other."

"Skin color comes in every shade, just like colors. A rainbow wouldn't be very pretty if some of the colors were left out."

Cultural Appropriation

Appropriation can be a very sensitive issue for people of color. In 2021, Black TikTok creators went on strike. Their creative dances and trends had received low views and were not promoted on the app. Once these original dances were taken and performed by White members, however, the TikTok algorithm showed the videos more often to more people and they earned higher views. Black creators were not credited with the dances. This may not seem like a big deal, but TikTok creators can become verified and earn revenue if they earn recognition and gain viewers. It's similar to how YouTubers can monetize their content and make a whole career on the platform.

In this way, Black people lose their creations and potential income—and this isn't a new phenomenon. After slavery ended, Black people were not allowed to perform on stage, so White people painted their faces black and played minstrel stereotypes, which were always offensive and one-dimensional. During the 1920s and 1930s, Black musicians signed appalling contracts and earned pennies for performances. Their music was later taken and remixed by White musicians—most notably Elvis, who did not give them credit.

Sports teams with Indigenous icons make millions, but it has taken decades of petitioning and lobbying by Indigenous people to get the offensive names and mascots changed. Non Indigenous people may still wear headdresses to music festivals or on Halloween, but they ignore issues on the reservations, such as missing women and girls, rampant alcoholism, the erasure of Indigenous culture, and the fact that people's relatives were forced from their homes a few centuries ago to live on small patches of land in the middle of the country.

The culture of Native Hawaiians and Pacific Islanders is underrepresented as tribal tattoos or grass skirts and leis, but do people know that Hawaii used to be a kingdom with its own constitution and language? It wasn't until US businessmen backed by the Marines took the country by force in an illegal overthrow that it became a US territory. The Hawaiian language, 'Ōlelo Hawai'i, became outlawed. Kānaka Maoli, or Native Hawaiians, possessed high literacy rates before occupation. Today, Kānaka

Maoli actively organize and fight for sovereignty and rights to their ancestral lands and cultural traditions.

Latino cultural appropriation includes racist Halloween costumes like sombreros and ponchos and acts of appropriation like White artists memorizing a few lines of Spanish to add to their songs.

White people have taken to wearing Japanese kimonos as morning robes and tattooing Chinese or Japanese characters on their bodies without knowing the meaning. Some of this appropriation stems from the history of US soldiers in Asian countries. This feeds into exoticism, which leads to the violence many Asian American women face.

So how can you keep cultural appropriation in check in the classroom?

Talk about meanings and encourage the use of appropriate names. For example, during Thanksgiving, do not make feathered headdresses. Make paper-hand turkeys instead. Encourage students to use the names of the actual tribes where you live. Discuss how they may not have celebrated Thanksgiving but how they may have given thanks.

Discourage inappropriate costumes. For example, send a letter home to parents before Halloween saying that certain costumes will respectfully not be allowed in class unless the child comes from that racial or ethnic background. These costumes include the following:

- Hawaiian grass skirts or leis
- Afros, faux dreads, and blackface
- Native American headdresses
- Sombreros and ponchos
- Sheik or Arab costumes
- Geisha costumes

Acknowledge and credit the original. Discuss how you can appreciate other cultures in a respectful way. Ask open-ended questions that stimulate discussion. Search for the origin of the content to give it proper credit. For example, the hand motion kids have picked up as they point to their elbow and say "Sheesh!" was popularized on TikTok, but it comes from NBA player D'Angelo Russell, who said he got the idea from his father who used to say "Ice in my veins" while Russell was growing up. "Ice in my veins" or "cold-blooded" are old, popular African American Vernacular English terms used in basketball for people who are calm under pressure.

Otherness in History: Savages and Exotics

When Whiteness becomes the "normal," people of color are looked at as "othered," and it becomes easy to dehumanize something that is othered. From the beginning of colonization, people of color have been fetishized into the categories of the exotic or the savage. These stereotypes each have their own harmful and pervasive roots, and they intersect when it comes to sexualizing minority women and girls.

Women throughout the US struggle to keep their rights to their bodies, are often blamed for assaults when they are the victims, and have to take daily safety measures to prevent becoming victims. Women of color find themselves with a distinct challenge to battle issues of gender and race concurrently. Historically, women of color were seen as less intelligent and less cultured than White women. They were profiled and stereotyped by their races, and they were seen as savages. That is, until they weren't, and then they became exotic.

Asian women can be labeled as subservient, quiet, and accommodating. They may be objectified, and men sometimes react with violence when Asian women do not stay quiet or fit the mold. This "mold" can also include the opposing idea of the hypersexual "dragon lady" who is supposed to please the White man. During wartime, American soldiers used Asian women as "comfort women." These were women and girls who were forced or sold into sexual slavery to be used by soldiers. Between 21–55 percent of Asian women have reported being physically or sexually assaulted, according to the Asian Pacific Institute on Gender-Based Violence. In the classroom, look out for phrases like "China doll" and jokes directed toward Asian kids about their mothers' professions. Because of COVID-19, look out for purposeful coughing directed at Asian students.

Latina women are stereotyped to have fiery tempers and large hips. Because of President Trump's anti-immigrant speeches and a general lack of accountability, hate crimes against Latino people have been on the rise. According to the FBI's 2019 Hate Crime Statistics, hate crimes rose by about 8 percent from 2018 to 2019. The number of instances stayed nearly the same for 2020 as well. In elementary school, be aware of jokes about marriage for green cards, comments about their developing bodies, or expectations for having many of their own children at a young age.

Black women are said to be aggressive, angry, and hypersexual. According to the National Center on Violence Against Women in the Black Community, one in four Black girls will be sexually assaulted before the age of 18, and 35 percent of Black women will experience sexual violence in their lives. In school, look for jokes about Black girls developing early, other kids telling girls to "twerk," or people saying that a Black girl is "acting grown." A Black girl does not "act grown" just because she wants to wear clothes like her mom or do her nails like her sister. Just like a White girl is not grown up because she wears yoga pants or goes to Starbucks with her sister.

Indigenous women's issues are often left unspoken and brushed away, but their silent struggles are distinct. Did you know that over five thousand Indigenous women and girls have been reported missing through the National Crime Information Center? These cases have suffered from a lack of thorough investigations due to communication and jurisdiction issues between federal, state, local, and tribal law enforcement.

Indigenous women and girls are at least three times more likely to be murdered than any other race or ethnicity, according to the Urban Indian Health Institute. The likelihood they will go missing is even higher. Over 80 percent of Indigenous women have experienced violence. More than half of these women have been sexually assaulted, according to the National Institute of Justice. Despite knowing all this, it wasn't until 2019 that the Missing and Murdered Unit within the Bureau of Indian Affairs Office of Justice Services was established to investigate and solve these cases.

According to the FBI's 2020 Hate Crimes Statistics, agencies reported a 32 percent increase from 2019 in hate crimes related to race and ethnicity.

In general, harassment against girls in elementary school looks like this:

- Pinching
- Pushing
- Hair pulling or cutting
- Skirt flipping

- Teasing about underclothes

- Joking about traditional female roles, e.g., "make me a sandwich"

- Using strength to restrain a girl in a casual manner, e.g., a handshake that turns into painful squeezing so the student cannot get her hand away

- Telling girls to smile or to be more feminine

- Filming girls without their permission

Note that this is not an exhaustive list.

How can you help your students?

- Report and intervene in instances of harassment.

- Promote self-defense and bodily autonomy.

- Teach boys and girls about consent to touch another person.

- Build self-confidence.

- Perform affirmations.

- Lead by example.

- Teach about great women leaders of all colors (shoot for three of each race at least).

Police and Prison Pipeline

Black parents have been having an uncomfortable talk with their kids for over a century about police officers. The talks start in elementary school, when kids are being taught about stranger danger and safe adults. Many Black kids are taught to be wary of police officers. While they are taught to call 911 in emergencies or if they are victims of a crime, Black kids are also taught to keep their hands out of their pockets when they approach officers. They are taught to approach slowly and to respond "Yes, sir" or "Yes, ma'am."

But this issue does not start with police contact. In fact, it starts in schools and with the difference BIPOC children face when it comes to punishments and reprimands. According to where you live, certain minority children are affected more than others. In states like Arizona and Texas, the Latino students see higher rates of punishment than their peers. In Hawaii, it is the Polynesian and Micronesian students. In certain cities, such as Chicago, it's Black students.

Keali'i Kukahiko, an institutional analyst at the Office of Hawaiian Education and a lecturer in the Department of Ethnic Studies at the University of Hawaii at Mānoa, has done extensive research on Hawaii's education system. During this time, he found similarities in the school-to-prison pipeline between Black Americans and Native Hawaiians. In a phone interview, he said, "The statistics for the discipline in compulsive education mirrored itself within the African American population at the prison level from juvenile incarceration to adult. What we found across the board for all of our achievement gaps in all four core subject areas, the leading indicator was cultural dissonance, not economic advantage."

Kukahiko has published several papers on how to improve Hawaiian education, including after the pandemic. In his research, he found that "not only were Native Hawaiians two to three times more likely than non-native Hawaiians to be identified for suspension, but our male special-ed Native Hawaiian Pacific Islanders were nine times more likely."

How does this affect students, and what does being identified for suspension mean? Kukahiko explained, "The suspension rates were a masking factor. When I looked at the data around suspension rates, there are obviously racial groups that are slightly higher. The conversation goes this way—'That's like six Native Hawaiians come in the principal's office and six get suspended. Ten White students come into the principal's office and five get suspended. Really it's just a difference of one.' No, it's not. Because when one hundred Native Hawaiians are getting identified but only 10 White students are identified, that's where the numbers start to become a problem. It's in the implicit bias."

This problem persists through the races. Students of color are identified more often as problem students. They are disciplined more often. They are reprimanded more often. They are scrutinized more often. This continual pressure and expectation of failure or bad behavior weighs on students of color. It changes their academic performance.

According to the American Civil Liberties Union, Black students who have been suspended are three times more likely to end up in contact with the juvenile justice system. Foster kids are even more likely to end up in the justice system, and once they are in, recidivism rates are high.

Private prisons profit off of prison labor, and the Thirteenth Amendment, which allows this profit, has been described as modern slavery. Netflix has an interesting documentary called *13th* on this subject.

How Can You Ensure Social Justice?

Employ restorative justice in your classroom. Restorative justice focuses on the healing of the victim rather than focusing on the perpetrator and their punishment. The good news is you've already started the process by examining your implicit biases. Then you checked for disparities when doling out consequences or punishments. When you next come back to the classroom, focus on mediation first instead of suspension or calls home. Call your student in for a discussion. Lastly, learn about cultural differences and switch communication tactics. If a student comes from a culture where eye contact is seen as a sign of respect, do not ask them to look at you when you talk to them. If a student communicates in a direct manner, try to not classify it as aggressive or rude.

Disciplining Students of Color

Exercise One: Take two weeks to review how often you discipline each student, including chastising or warnings. Really get into it. Write down the students' names and their consequences for each action.

Who is getting talked to the most? Who is sitting in a cozy corner or time out the most? Who is getting the phone calls home or the emails to their parents?

Are the students minorities? It wouldn't be a surprise. Black preschoolers are 2.5 percent more likely to be suspended than their White counterparts, according to the US Department of Education Office of Civil Rights. This trend continues throughout elementary and secondary school, but it is not because Black children are more challenging or more ready to break rules than anyone else. In a 2016 study from the Yale School of Medicine, teachers were told to watch clips of four students in order to look out for "challenging behaviors," and eye-trackers found that teachers watched the Black boys 42 percent of the time, much more than any of the other three kids. Surprise, surprise, there were actually no challenging behaviors in the video.

Black boys are also perceived to be older than their peers by as much as four years, according to a 2014 study published in American Psychological Association's Journal of Personality and Social Psychology. This means that a nine-year-old Black boy is treated as if he were a teenager. People put expectations on his behavior as if he were much older than he is. (This perception also leads back to the idea of the poverty trap and the exploitative prison system, since Black boys are 18 times more likely to be tried as adults than White boys who committed the same offense, according to co-founder of the Center for Policing Equity Phillip Atiba Goff. He is also a professor of African American Studies and Psychology at Yale University).

Exercise Two: When you see a student of color acting out, reframe your thinking. Ask yourself if the behavior is really interrupting the class or interrupting just your perception of how class should run. Let's say Anthony is standing at the back of the classroom instead of sitting. He is leaning over his desk and doing his work. He is supposed to be sitting in his chair like everyone else. Isn't it OK that he is standing? His work is getting done. Don't some people in offices have standing desks?

Is a child misbehaving or just excited? Kids are impulsive, and sometimes it is hard to walk to recess. Can you instruct the whole class instead to join you in tiptoeing to recess like spies or waddling like ducks in a row?

How would you react if it was a White child? How did you last react when a White child did this? Didn't John just get out of his seat to ask you a question two minutes ago? You listened to him, answered his question, and told him next time to raise his hand. Aaron is now out of his seat at his buddy's desk. Maybe he is asking for help, or maybe he is answering a question. Ask if you can help the pair. Remind Aaron in the same gentle way to raise his hand next time. Then perhaps self-examine why Aaron or his buddy did not feel comfortable asking you for help directly.

Is it a cultural difference? Are they talking out of turn, or are they hyping up another student who gave a correct answer?

Common Microaggressions

You may hear microaggressions coming from your students in the classroom, or you may use them yourself without knowing. Remember that the important thing is to call people in, focus on restorative justice, and use knowledge or education as the most powerful tool.

These are not innocent questions:

- Where are you from?
- How did your parents meet?
- Do you speak a second language?
- What's your real name?

This may seem counterintuitive when you're trying to learn more about other people and other races, but these questions or comments happen too frequently in the life of a person of color. They are frustrating questions and make the person of color feel "othered" when they are also American. Students know what you're really asking about is their race so they can fit into one of the boxes in your brain.

These are not compliments:

- You speak English so well./You're so articulate./You don't sound Black./You don't have an accent.
- You're so _____ for a _____./You're so pretty for a Black girl./You're so funny for an Asian kid.
- I bet you're good at _____./I bet you're good at math./I bet you're good at basketball.

Students are individuals with distinct personalities and feelings. While children are shaped by their families and cultures around them, your students are also being raised in the US. US culture is also their culture. They have more to them than their race, just like you have more to you than your race.

Colorblindness is not good, and comments like these are not productive:

- When I look at you, I don't see color.

- There is only the human race.

- You could be black or White or yellow or purple. I would treat you the same.

Colorblindness is the idea that you don't see race. It's the idea that you don't treat people differently because of their race. This well-intentioned idea is very harmful because—as it says in the name—it turns a blind eye to issues of color. But, you need to erase colorblindness to see the whole student. After a two-year investigation into colorblind policy at a Utah school, the lead researchers, Nancy Ares and Edward Buendia, wrote that "a color-blind focus on students as individuals constrains educators' abilities to respond to students' experiences as members of social, cultural, and linguistic groups, ignoring their differential treatment in schools and in the larger world."

There is still racism in the US and the world. There are still people that hold onto implicit biases and act accordingly. There are still policies in place that push down the success of minorities. The inequality needs to be seen so that it can be fixed. Your students want you to see the whole of them, not only their racial stereotypes but also not without the racial context that surrounds them.

In *The Guide for White Women Who Teach Black Boys*, teacher Debby Irving says, "I entered teaching fancying myself colorblind, and therefore able to love and teach each student equally. The truth, however, is that I did see color." She goes on to talk about how she envisioned herself fixing and helping the minority students. She now recognizes those ideas came from her own entitlement and savior complex. She tells a story about how she crushed the spirit of a Haitian girl several times in her effort to help the girl complete her work. Only near the end of the year did Irving realize that there was a difference in cultural values and that the Haitian girl was not wrong in her actions, only different. In her essay, she reflects on how, if she was given the chance to change her past, she would become more culturally aware before entering the classroom.

Erase these from your vocabulary and inner dialogue:

- Saying or thinking "you people"

- Imitating accents

- Saying or thinking "I can fix/save these students"

Even young students will start to pick up on speech patterns. They may see outdated/classic comedies with accents or hear the adults around them adapt these phrases. Discourage this and instead encourage learning the actual language or how to have the flexibility of mind to understand the English language through the lens of an accent.

Stop thinking that you can't be racist because of these reasons:

- You have Black friends.

- Your kids/husband is Black.

- You're a woman so you know what it's like to be marginalized.

- You're Black/Latino/Asian.

The only good follow-up to "I can't be racist because" should be "I recognize my racist beliefs and I am working to get rid of them."

We live in a time in which students have become advocates and will call out one another on racist, sexist, and classist ideas. They will even call out parents and teachers. Instead of getting defensive, the person who was called out should ask why the student thinks that, reflect on what was said, and think about how to be better in the future. The person doing the calling out should make sure to use the phrase "racist ideas" or "implicit biases" because the person on the receiving end is less likely to feel attacked and get defensive. When you phrase it as if that person with racist ideas is the victim, you are more likely to make progress with them. For example, saying, "You were probably taught this without even knowing," or, "You might have picked it up from your community growing up," may make someone less defensive.

My mom, a White woman who had five mixed-Black children, would push back any time we pointed out her racist ideas. One time she said that our old neighborhood was going downhill, and it was good we moved when we did. She said this as she pointed out the many Black people who had moved in. As her children, it made us feel bad about the Black parts of ourselves. When we pointed out this racist idea years later, our intentions were to make ourselves feel seen and to open her eyes so she could get rid of those implicit biases she was probably taught as a kid.

You can find a good reference PDF online that contains a table of common microaggressions in the article "Racial Microaggressions in Everyday Life: Implications for Clinical Practice" from the journal *American Psychologist*.

SECTION II

THE SPECIFIC

While no community is a monolith, it is important to know the stereotypes or racist ideas specific children face.

Ernest J. Wilson III is a professor at the University of Southern California who founded the Center for Third Space Thinking. He teaches and researches soft skills, or survival skills, to businesses and organizations; his core soft skills are adaptability, cultural competence, empathy, intellectual curiosity, and 360-degree thinking.

Wilson said, "Issues of diversity, exclusion, racism, homophobia, and gender attacks are serious, and these teachings that we try to do need to be nuanced. Those of us that are educators can't put our heads in the sand and pretend that these differences don't exist. We want our children to be healthy and adaptable and culturally empathetic, and that may take extra time." He went on to warn that "the cost of not doing that, without being too dramatic, is that the US could be driven apart. That's not something nice to leave for our children or grandchildren or great-grandchildren."

Stereotypes and racism are designed to pull people apart and put them in boxes. Traits or implicit biases are not correct, but they are attributed to certain groups so frequently that these groups have found themselves battling specific issues, like the idea that Asians are good at math. This stereotype plays into the model minority myth, which falsely elevates Asian Americans as the model that all minorities should strive to follow. The myth sews distrust and animosity between racial groups, ignores systemic oppression that makes this mythological success nearly impossible, and denies the struggles Asian Americans have due to their race. This often leads to assumptions of family values and a blindness to areas in which a student may need more support. I will further examine this specific example in Chapter 6.

Chapter 3

BLACK

This section addresses barriers and stereotypes that Black students face in the classroom. The Black community is not a monolith and, while Black is the most accepted term right now, some people still use African American. This should not be confused with African immigrant students or first-generation African students. Another term for Black people right now is African diaspora, which are peoples and communities specifically descended from slaves.

Hair

You've seen it on the news and in documentaries. You've seen it in the magazines and in feature films. Black people love their hair. White people try to copy it and get called out for cultural appropriation because, well, it's appropriation. What you might not know is that a stigma against Black people's hair started during slavery.

Black people brought to the US were bought and sold as commodities or livestock. Many times, their African cultural practices, dances, and hairstyles were banned. In some instances, their hair was cut off to be used alongside cotton or wool for cushioning in items like beds and chairs. They were treated literally like livestock. Shorn and sent back to the fields. The hair styles Black people were allowed to keep were called protective styles, which kept the sun off the scalp and kept hair out of their faces. The styles were easy to clean and manage since slaves had limited time for themselves.

After Emancipation and Juneteenth, White people's hair was looked at as "good hair" and Black hair was looked at as bad and foreign. To become more attractive to employers and to "fit in" in the US, Black people started to use hot irons, sew-ins, and wigs to have straight hair. Chemical straighteners were created. After nearly a century, there was a push to be able to wear natural hair like afros, locs, and cornrows in the 1960s and 1970s. During this time, many Black people were fired from their employment because their hair was deemed unprofessional. Black students were also punished for hair that did not fit the dress code because it was a "distraction."

Today, there is a big push for natural hair and respecting cultures, so it may seem like all of this is old news. However, people in power still hold these views. When I was a teenager, I had a job as a childcare team member at a bougie, White-collar gym, and I was told during orientation that I could not wear "dreads" because it was seen as unprofessional and dirty. I had never worn dreadlocks, but I was not surprised. It was not the last time an employer censored my hair.

Dreadlocks got their name because of the negative connotation of the word "dread." Today, it is becoming more common to refer to this style of hair as just locs.

In classrooms and businesses today, there are still so many misconceptions about Black hair and Black hairstyles. The Tableau of Hair chart shows some things you might hear from kids and possible responses supported by facts.

The "Stereotype" column shows the phrase you may hear a student or another teacher say. The "Response" column is a short response you can give. If there is pushback or someone asks for more information, the "Explanation" column provides you background information so that you can respond from a place of knowledge.

Tableau of Hair

Stereotype	Response	Explanation
It's dirty.	It's not.	It is washed, yes, even the locs. Black hair is washed on a different schedule than White hair. In general, Black hair dries out faster. It doesn't get as oily, so it does not need to be shampooed every day, but that doesn't mean it's not washed.
It's not natural.	It grows out of people's heads like that.	The straight black hair that you see on Black women comes from wigs or an extreme chemical called relaxer that is usually combined with a flat iron. It's very damaging to hair and can cause chemical burns to the head.

Tableau of Hair

Stereotype	Response	Explanation
It's a distraction.	It's not, and it wouldn't be one if it was normalized as it should be.	Kids like what's new, but as you know, they quickly grow bored. Natural hair used to be policed—and sometimes still is—in school and business dress codes. Black people are finally feeling comfortable enough to wear their hair naturally and express their culture, like the Irish do on St. Patrick's Day or women's being allowed to wear pants. Once it's normalized, it's not a distraction.
You can touch it.	No. Don't touch it.	Don't ask to touch it either. Besides the fact that touching or pulling the hair could mess up the style, Black hair and Black bodies are not exotic toys.
It's not real.	It could be. Black hair comes in many styles and lengths and types of curl.	Black hair can be natural or in a protective style or extensions or a wig or anything in between. People have often asked if my hair is real because of how it can change in appearance. I wear my hair naturally and even then it can appear longer or shorter depending on where I am in the wash cycle or how I slept on it. A good rule of thumb: unless we are talking about hair and it is a two-way conversation, it's not something to comment on.

Tableau of Hair

Stereotype	Response	Explanation
It's like a poodle.	Nope. Do not compare the hair of a person to the hair of an animal. Not a dog or a sheep or anything like that.	Black people are not animals. It would not be a compliment if someone said to a White person, "Wow, your hair is so flat and oily like cooked spaghetti." This is also offensive because there is a history of White people treating Black people like livestock. See the text above.
It's nappy.	It's not nappy. That's an offensive word.	It's curly, kinky, frizzy, or downy. There are several types of curly hair and most Black hair falls between 3b and 4c types, according to the Andre Walker Hair Classification System.
It's a bird's/rat nest. I could hide my pencil in there.	Don't hide anything in there. It's not a nest. This is offensive.	Sometimes your hair doesn't have a good day. You wouldn't want someone to point it out and then make a joke of it.
You should run a comb through it/cut it/take these braids out.	Never touch or cut or comb Black hair without a parent's permission.	Unless you are a stylist that specializes in Black hair, do not touch or cut or comb a student's hair. Braids can last weeks, and they are expensive and time consuming to put in. You also cannot comb or cut Black hair the same way White hair is done.

Tableau of Hair

Stereotype	Response	Explanation
Cornrows/ beads are so ghetto.	Braids are protective styles rooted in Black history.	Cornrows and beaded braids are styles that do not need many, if any, daily touch-ups. They can help hair grow and keep the hair and scalp safe from the elements.

What can you say about Black hair? Find something that is objective and not a comparison.

- Wow, those beads are cool.
- I like your hairstyle!
- How long did it take to get your braids done? You must be great at sitting still.
- Your curls are awesome.

Or don't compliment the hair. Compliment anything outside of a child's Black body, like their shoes or clothes or backpack or the way they high five. Compliment their sweater or the way they organize their colored pencils or the character on their T-shirt.

Code Switching

I debated putting this section here because other communities also do code switching. Code switching is alternating between two languages depending on the audience, but in Black daily life, this can also apply to the culture. Black culture is reflected in handshakes and head nods. It's in the way Black people speak English—known as African American Vernacular English (AAVE) or Black Vernacular English (BVE)—when speaking with family or friends. AAVE is also where much popular slang comes from, and many times it becomes popularized after it is appropriated by White culture.

Very often AAVE isn't recognized as its own language, and teachers will try to prepare Black students for the "real world" by correcting their language or asking them to speak "proper" English. Yes, Black children do need to learn to code switch, and some strategies for encouraging this are better than others.

Wilson told me that in his elementary school days in Washington, DC, before desegregation, all his teachers were Black. His teachers knew the importance of code switching. "It meant that they gave us cues and responses and warnings about how to behave or [what to] look out for," said Wilson. He further explained that teachers should be educated on cultural competency for the good of all students. He stated, "The evidence that I have seen suggests that having a teacher of the same cultural background leads to better performance outcomes for students, especially students of color. If that is true, then we are sending teachers into their first professional settings with a deficiency that needs to be addressed. That's a disservice to everybody."

When having students answer questions, specify when it should be in American English. If you are a teacher coming into a neighborhood where AAVE is the primary spoken language, be mindful of your requests. You are a guest in their neighborhood. Also, avoid using phrases like "proper English" to describe American English.

Discuss language in context. Some kids may know about code switching already. For those who don't, explain that it is like learning a different language. By learning American English alongside AAVE, they can master how they appear or sound to people outside their neighborhood. It's like how people that speak two or more languages have an easier time traveling to a different country. As an exercise, have students brainstorm other advantages or scenarios of speaking two languages or of speaking AAVE and American English. It could be as simple as speaking AAVE to a grandparent who never graduated from high school while waiting in line at a grocery store and then talking to the cashier in American English.

Code switch in the classroom. Make a chart of exchanges. When a student says a phrase like "out of pocket" and you don't know the meaning, ask them what it means. Then ask how else they could phrase that saying. Add each phrase to its appropriate side of the chart. Refer and add to the chart throughout the school year. Again, avoid using phrases like "proper English" to describe American English.

AAVE	American English
No cap	No lie, telling the truth
You gon be	You're going to be
Finna/fixin/fittin	Getting ready to/about to

Get a dictionary. For older elementary students, if the book *Frindle* by Andrew Clements is still on the curriculum, check out how the English language has evolved over the last few years. What slang has been added to the official dictionary? What words have become "real" words? What is the history of these words?

Bring languages to life. Share videos of other versions of the English language like Spanglish, Cajun/Creole, Southern, British English, and Hawaiian Pidgin. Can students understand what's being said? Where did these languages/accents/dialects come from? How did they develop? Wired has a great two-part video on this topic online called "Accent Expert Gives a Tour of US Accents" that features language experts and labels each accent/dialect found throughout the US.

Chapter 4

INDIGENOUS AMERICAN

This chapter has been titled "Indigenous American" because there is no one widely accepted term for this population. According to the Native Knowledge 360 program at the Smithsonian's National Museum of the American Indian, "Native American" is becoming an outdated term. Most people that fall into this category prefer their own tribal name when it is known. American Indian is still widely accepted and, in Canada, so is First Nations. Sometimes you can better localize a native population like Alaskan Native or Hawaiian.

> In Hawaii, it is respectful to leave the term "Hawaiian" for people of actual Hawaiian descent and not just anyone who comes from or lives in the state. Hawaii resident and islander are the more proper terms for people who live in the state but do not have Native Hawaiian ancestors.

Like every race, no tribe of Indigenous Americans can speak for the whole. No single tribe is a marker for all the cultural differences that make up native peoples. In fact, there are 574 federally recognized tribes. This section covers some of the overlapping issues Indigenous Americans face, such as offensive stereotypes, erasure of history, and reservation life.

The Stereotypes

Here's a list of a few stereotypes that Indigenous kids may face in the classroom. These are the most common, but the list is not exhaustive. The chart also includes responses and explanations you can use if you hear a student or another teacher say these things. Use your judgment when speaking to young students as to how much to include when it comes to heavy topics like rape and war.

You May Have Heard

The Stereotype: My great-grandmother was a Cherokee princess.

The Response: Probably not. This is a common myth that's passed through families.

The Explanation: Unless you can trace your family ancestry to a particular person that belonged to a specific tribe, you are probably not Cherokee or even native.

Sometimes light-skin Black individuals wrote themselves down as American Indians to avoid being labeled and stereotyped as Black. Other times, people mistook ancestors from India as their "Indian princess" heritage. Still further, White people with skin that tans easily or that have ambiguous features, leaned into the "native royalty" myth. Some people who have looked into their ancestry have learned that their "exotic princess" was the child born from the rape of a slave.

***

The Stereotype: American Indians have red skin./I burn and get red skin because I have American Indian blood in me.

The Response: The use of the term "redskin" is offensive, and American Indians do not have red skin. They have a shade of brown like most other people in the world.

The Explanation: "Redskin" was used as the identifier because "black" was already taken by Black people. For the most part, people who referred to American Indians as red were White people.

Sometimes in the past, redskin referred to the literal bloody scalps from American Indians' heads that White settlers would turn in for rewards after killing them. There is debate that some American Indians also scalped their enemies, and that is the reason they were called redskin. Also, some tribes, like the Beothuk of Newfoundland, used red ochre tones to paint their bodies.

Either way, White skin does not turn red in the sun because a person is part American Indian. More likely, they are not American Indian at all and their skin is turning red because they aren't wearing enough sunscreen.

***

The Stereotype: They live in teepees./They live in grass huts./They live in igloos.

The Response: Like people everywhere today, Indigenous people live in a variety of homes, including apartments, single-family houses, brick houses, and condos.

The Explanation: Teepees are a type of dwelling specific to Indigenous peoples of the Great Plains. Grass huts are a type of dwelling specific to Native Hawaiians. It is their culture and their history.

Culture and history may be preserved in structures; for example, the Roman Colosseum is still preserved, but it is not used as it once was.

Indigenous people do not still live like that. Like every other race in the US, most have access to running water and electricity.

***

The Stereotype: They were uncivilized savages that wore loincloths.

The Response: Not at all. Their cultures and customs may have been different, but they had their own languages, histories, and cities, just like Europeans.

Their outfits were as varied as the number of tribes. Like White people, their clothing came from animal products. American Indians used hides, while White immigrants used wool.

The Explanation: A different culture made them no more or less civilized than anyone else. One of the reasons that the large cities were not "discovered" was because disease had wiped out millions of people. These people did not have bad immune systems. While they literally did not have immunity to these kinds of microbes before; raids and enslavement created a superhighway for the spreading of disease. Tribes were left underpopulated with no one to take care of the sick.

The White immigrants that came to the Americas also had different ideas and values that they chose to use as a lens with which to see a whole group of people.

***

The Stereotype: A lot of American Indians do drugs, drink alcohol, or smoke substances.

The Response: This is a stereotype that comes from the issues of alcoholism on reservations. It is not true of all American Indians.

The Explanation: Alcohol use among American Indians is significantly higher than other ethnic groups, according to American Addiction Centers and the National Institutes of Health. The reasons behind this are long and varied, and they stem from the introduction of alcohol by White immigrants.

Not all American Indians drink or indulge in drugs. This idea that they do has been dangerously applied to missing Indigenous women and children. Police often miss the crucial first 24 hours of an investigation because they excuse the absence as "The woman is out partying," or "She ran away."

Conversely, many White Americans try drugs and drink alcohol in their teenage, young adult, and adult lives, and this behavior is not associated with White Americans except with "poor White trash."

***

The Stereotype: They own casinos now, so they at least get back at the White man.

The Response: There are such things as tribal casinos, and their revenue is supposed to go to the reservation that owns that land.

Casinos and gaming have been profitable for some tribes. For others, it has not worked to stimulate the economy.

The Explanation: Because reservations are treated as sovereign nations, they can make their own laws and hold their own courts. They even have their own law enforcement.

Due to this sovereignty, tribal nations are able to have casinos and gambling even in states where it is illegal. Sometimes this has been profitable and has stimulated the tribal economy by creating jobs and increasing revenue to improve health care or education. However, location of the reservation and other issues impact the success in some cases.

Also, American Indians do not own every casino in the US, and some of the tribal casinos aren't even native owned.

***

The Stereotype: Hawaii is paradise.

The Response: While Hawaii is a great place to vacation, the idea that it is paradise minimizes the struggles that many native families and people of color have faced since the Hawaiian Kingdom was overthrown by US businessmen.

The Explanation: Hawaii used to be paradise, in a sense. During the time of the Hawaiian Kingdom, literacy rates were high, and the native population fished and grew crops using sustainable methods.

After the arrival of White sailors, disease started to spread. Mosquitoes came over as well as other invasive species like rats and mice. These things destroyed Hawaii's ecosystem.

After American citizens took over, they stole land and forbade native customs, including the Hawaiian language. Many people in Hawaii today still struggle to feed their families as a result of this. Households are multigenerational, and it takes several incomes just to cover a mortgage and utilities. Affording food and other imported goods can be a struggle because everything has to be shipped, and the island relies on tourism as its main economy. Hawaii is no longer self-sustainable.

***

The Stereotype: Hawaiian hula girls wore coconuts on their breasts, grass skirts, and no shoes.

The Response: Hula is an important Polynesian cultural dance. Different forms with different styles of dress are performed throughout the Polynesian Islands, including Hawaii. Men and women perform hula. And hula performances have different meanings.

The Explanation: It is important not to sexualize all hula. The performances have their own meanings and require many years of study to get it right. Some hula is for the gods. Other performances were for dignitaries or royalty or served as prayers.

While women in the past did perform topless or with coconut bras, they no longer do that. Missionaries thought it was a heathen dance and convinced Hawaiian royalty to ban it.

Hawaiian culture and attitudes toward sex and nudity were very different than Western standards.

There are also some positive stereotypes like the "wise elder" and the "helpful sidekick." While these two ideas are rooted in history, they are not the whole story. People are people. They have whole stories, and they are their own main characters.

Wise Elder

In these cultures, it is common to look toward an elder for guidance. There are, however, young people also taking a stand for their land, their customs, and their languages. Some elders belong to a time when it was common to take native children from their homes and put them with White families to "civilize" them or assimilate them into US culture. In this way, some elders are relearning their own culture now that they are free to do so.

Sidekick

Sometimes a young genius or an overeager helper, the sidekick is a popular trope for American Indians. It minimizes their real story, one outside of who they are besides a helping hand. The most popular form of this character can be seen in Tonto in the old westerns. There's the fairy tale that American Indians were helpful to the White immigrants. They helped them navigate the country and talk to other tribes. They taught White people to farm and to discern what was safe to eat. They shared food. The American Indians willingly gave up their land so the White people had a place to stay. They learned English so they could act as ambassadors to other tribes for explorers.

A lot of these assumptions are either half-truths or completely untrue. One of the most famous sidekicks, Sacagawea, accompanied Lewis and Clark as they explored the Louisiana Territory. You might imagine a young adult who stepped up to volunteer to navigate so she could also explore that country. Not quite. She had been captured by another tribe at the age of 12 and then sold to a White trader/explorer named Toussaint Charbonneau at age 13. Charbonneau wanted to get hired for the expedition and told Lewis and Clark that Sacagawea spoke Shoshone. The explorers made her go with them on the voyage even though she had just given birth to Charbonneau's son.

Another real-life twist occurs in the story of Squanto, who helped translate between White immigrants from the Mayflower and native tribes in the area. His real name was actually Tisquantum, and he had been kidnapped from his tribe by Captain Thomas Hunt after he and some fellow men had been invited to the ship to view items to trade. Hunt betrayed them and stuffed them below deck. Squanto was then going to be sold into slavery until friars blocked the sale. At the time, Spanish law said that American Indians could not be sold in the slave trade. After four years, Squanto learned enough

English that he offered to translate for a ship if they would take him back to his home. When he got back to his tribe, he realized they had all been decimated by disease.

Many of these stereotypes are due to colonization. Colonization can be defined as the destruction of native populations and customs in order for European and Western powers to benefit politically or economically. Colonialism is the policy behind it. Sometimes this policy was hidden under the agenda of spreading Christianity or protecting freedoms. Sometimes it was just done to extend the reach of the empires of England and Spain.

Regardless of the reasons behind it, colonization always brought certain effects with it:

- Erasure of native customs, languages, and religions
- Disease
- Violence against native people
- Seizure of native lands
- Racism
- Subjugation if not enslavement
- Sexual assault of Indigenous women by White immigrants

Native populations today still feel the aftereffects of these hostile takeovers.

Barriers to Equity

Misinformation

There is an idea that the White immigrants and a random American Indian tribe came together to share a Thanksgiving meal. The name of the tribe was actually the Wampanoag, and their relationship with the immigrants was more of a political alliance. While the Wampanoag did help the immigrants to have a successful harvest and did partake in a fall harvest together, it all fell apart after the immigrants continued to violate the agreements they had made with the Wampanoag. Instead of focusing on this fairy tale of Thanksgiving, teach about your local American Indian tribe or the people who lived on the land before it was settled by White immigrants.

Then you can also teach about the concept of giving thanks. The Smithsonian's National Museum of the American Indian has an educator resource on the Native Knowledge 360 website called "Rethinking Thanksgiving Celebrations: Native Perspectives on Thanksgiving" that includes posters and activities.

On Columbus Day, many people now celebrate Indigenous Peoples' Day. Celebrate the people that lived in the US before White people arrived. Within 130 years of the first contact from Europeans, nearly 95 percent of the American Indian population was gone because of disease and race-based warfare. It is insulting to celebrate Christopher Columbus when he and the men under his command enslaved American Indians, tortured and mutilated Indigenous people, and raped women and girls.

Did you know that Columbus wasn't the first White man to land in the Americas? Colonel Charles Whittlesey wrote notes in the 1800s claiming that "five and six hundred years before the arrival of Columbus, the Northmen sailed from Norway, Iceland, and Freeland along the Atlantic coast as far as Long Island. They found Indian tribes, in what is now New England, closely resembling those who lived upon the coast and the St. Lawrence when the French and English came to possess these regions."

Erasure on the Mainland

Many Indigenous populations have dealt with erasure of their histories, customs, religions, and even languages due to colonization. Through laws and bans and violence, Indigenous people had their voices suppressed. Their original lands were seized.

I went to my local library and found an old book published in 1881 titled *History of Summit County, Ohio*. It gives a brief history of Ohio that includes information on the native people that lived there, and it describes the Iroquois as "monsters of the wilderness" for being at war with their neighbors. Most of the time, the Indigenous people of Ohio are called "savages" or "red man" when their tribal name is not used.

The book then describes how the land of Ohio came to be: "No sooner had the Americans obtained control of this country than they began, by treaty and purchase, to acquire the lands of the natives. 'The true basis of title to Indian territory is the right of civilized men to the soil for purposes of cultivation.' The same maxim may be applied to all uncivilized nations."

So, through word choice, it establishes that the native people were savages and—without directly saying it—uncivilized people who did not have a right to the land. As the story continues, the Indigenous people profess friendship with the White immigrants and continue to give up their land even though they have "jealous eyes."

Except it wasn't always peaceful. Later in this same book, it describes border wars in which "the daring and intrepidity of many of these Indian slayers was astonishing. They seemed to delight in the awful work and courted death and torture with reckless courage that arouses the keenest interest of those who read of their exploits. Hundreds of Indians were killed without any pretext, save the sport afforded the intrepid borderers, or to avenge wrongs done by the savage."

Then, with caucasity, the writer describes the scene after the War of 1812: "Savage men, like savage beasts, are engaged in continual migrations. Now, none are left. The White man occupies the home of the red man."

"Caucasity" is a BVE term for "audacity" for white people. A mixture of "Caucasian" and "audacity".

For mainland American Indians, their ancestors were forcibly assimilated or placed into the "empty" middle of the US to be forgotten. Yet there was still routine government interference. As people moved west, the US government made an effort to have American bison killed off so that American Indians lacked a crucial food source. This effort has been nicknamed "The Buffalo War."

During the gold rush in California, the US government forced American Indian tribes to sign treaties to give up rights to traditional lands and then concealed these treaties until an investigation by the Northern California Indian Association in 1905. Some of these treaties went back to 1851. Activist groups sought compensation in the 1940s, and they won over $50 million.

By the 1960s, at least three out of every 10 American Indian children were taken away from their families to be raised by White families or government boarding schools. These children were sometimes as young as five. Families were torn apart, and the children did not get to learn the traditions and customs of their heritage.

The Indian Child Welfare Act (ICWA) was passed in 1978 and designated that tribes can act as parents when a child needs to be removed from the home. Preference should be given to native people when adopting native children from the foster system. However, this federal law often remains ignored by caseworkers. The ICWA is currently being challenged in the Supreme Court.

Indigenous women and girls that stay on the reservation still go missing, and it has been that way for decades. Their disappearances remained unsolved in part due to federal, state, and tribal law enforcement agencies not working together. To combat this, the Bureau of Indian Affairs recently established the Missing and Murdered Unit to investigate these cases. But American Indian women are still subject to high levels of violence from non-Indigenous men. The federal courts have the ability to prosecute these men but have not done so consistently.

In terms of tribal rights, tribes have had to take their cases to the supreme courts when attempting to manage their own land on the reservation. Federal courts have affirmed several times that tribal reservations can act as sovereign nations, but individual states still try to impose restrictions. This is made more difficult because not all federally recognized tribes have reservation land. Some tribes are only recognized at the state level and are therefore not protected by the federal government.

Erasure in Alaska

Russia entered Alaska in the early 1700s and began fur trading and marine hunting. Sometimes interactions with the tribes were peaceful. Other times, Indigenous people were enslaved, kidnapped, and/or sold into slavery. Specifically, the Aleut people were targeted, and within 50 years, they lost 80 percent of their population to disease from Russian contact.

The pillaging of natural resources quickly became unsustainable, but Indigenous men were conscripted from their villages under threat of violence. They were sent farther and farther away to hunt and supply goods for trade. In the meantime, Russian men moved in and began to marry Indigenous women. The children of these marriages were educated by Russian missionaries and then often sent to Russia to further their education.

In 1867, the US purchased Alaska from Russia. US colonialism took hold, and Jim Crow-type segregation laws were applied to the Indigenous people. Schools were segregated and Alaskan Natives were not allowed to vote until 1915—and then only if they gave up their cultures and customs.

During World War II, about nine hundred Unangax from the Aleutian Islands were removed from their land due to the possibility of the area's becoming a combat zone, or so the US military said. White Americans living in the same area were not forced to leave. In fact, there was a search to find everyone who was at least one-eighth Unangax for removal. During the process, many elderly and children died because of how poorly it was handled. When those that survived returned, they found their homes had been looted. Today, these people are called Aleuts.

In 1959, Alaska became a state. By 1971, the Alaska Native Claims Settlement Act returned land to Alaskan Natives but not in the way of reservations. It established 13 regional profitable corporations and two hundred village corporations. Alaskan Natives were given stock in these. The act has been revised several times and has several other complex aspects. While it has remained largely positive, there are some criticisms because stocks can be sold to non-native corporations.

Erasure in Hawaii

Hawaii used to be the Kingdom of Hawaii with recognition from European countries. The kingdom was a strong trading partner for the US. It had its own official, written language; public schooling; and high literacy rates. It had its own legislation and court system. The US began to lease Pearl Harbor in January 1887 because of its strategic placement in the Pacific. It had been pressuring the kingdom for years to use it for military purposes and as an intermediary for trade. Then, a few months later, non-native Hawaiians rebelled and forced King Kalākaua under threat of assassination to sign a constitution the rebels had written in 1887. It is known as the Bayonet Constitution because of the threat of violence that came with it. This document stripped the monarchy of its power and created a wealthy, non-native legislature. The constitution also gave voting rights to wealthy noncitizens and restricted voting access for Native Hawaiians. It also excluded Asian citizens from voting.

After the King died in 1891, his sister took the throne. Queen Liliʻuokalani tried to rewrite the constitution to give back the power to the native people, but she was overthrown in 1893 by a group calling itself the Committee of Safety. The 13 members were US citizens backed by US and European businessmen.

Initially, President Grover Cleveland refused to officially annex Hawaii. Despite the fact that the House of Representatives accepted the treaty for annexation, President Cleveland believed that the US acted shamefully.

In a message to Congress, President Cleveland wrote, "By an act of war, committed with the participation of a diplomatic representative of the US and without authority of Congress, the Government of a feeble but friendly and confiding people has been overthrown. A substantial wrong has thus been done which a due regard for our national character as well as the rights of the injured people requires we should endeavor to repair."

The president withdrew the treaty from the Senate and tried to restore the queen to power, but the US public did not support it. Hawaii did not become a US territory until 1898, when President William McKinley signed it into law. In the meantime, the Hawaiian language was banned from being taught in schools in 1896.

Hawaii eventually gained statehood in 1959. In the 1960s and 1970s, there was a resurgence of the Hawaiian language and cultural practices with provisions being created during the Hawaii State Constitutional Convention in 1978. In 1993, Congress formally apologized for the overthrow of the Hawaiian monarchy.

In 2000, Senator Daniel Akaka proposed the Native Hawaiian Government Reorganization Act to give Native Hawaiians federal recognition similar to American Indians on the mainland. Known as the Akaka Bill, several iterations of this bill have been proposed since then. Many Native Hawaiians oppose it because they believe it still does not make up for the overthrow of their government. They do not want to compromise on their sovereignty.

Native Hawaiians still struggle today. A March 2018 report from the State of Hawaii's Department of Business, Economic Development and Tourism found that Native Hawaiians have the highest poverty rates among all the races in Hawaii. Hawaii's housing market outprices its residents, which causes multiple generations of families to live in one home. Since the economy is reliant on tourism and imported goods, it has been severely impacted by COVID-19. Low wages make underemployment and multiple jobs a way of life.

Keali'i Kukahiko, the education expert from Chapter 2, found research to indicate, however, that mainly racial background, rather than wealth, affects educational achievement in Hawaii.

"When we look at low-SES [socioeconomic status] Native Hawaiian Pacific Islanders and low-SES non-native Hawaiian Pacific Islanders, the non-native Hawaiian Pacific Islanders had almost double the scores of the Native Hawaiian Pacific Islanders," he reported.

Going Forward

Today, native traditions are being revitalized and Indigenous populations are pushing back against inequity. Hawaii officially has more than one language—and it is the only state officially to do so. Hawaii's languages are English, Hawaiian, and Pidgin. Nā Hopena Aʻo is an Office of Hawaiian Education (OHE) policy to develop skills unique to Hawaii, like the language and culture. If you are a teacher in Hawaii, learn some Hawaiian and really take time to pronounce street names and cities correctly. Nā Hopena Aʻo also assists teachers with lesson plans, material requests, and questions about integrating into their unique communities.

Kukahiko wants a new framework for education to explicitly optimize outcomes for belonging, responsibility, excellence, aloha, total well-being, and Hawaii. Right now, he said, there is a problem with compulsory education that started with the colonization of Hawaii and continues today.

> The whole market-based compulsory education was meant to civilize and domesticate a people through a single narrative. And that single narrative still exists. It continues to measure our kids by standards of success that are not right. It's perpetuated because we continue to buy online curriculum from Florida, Ohio, and Oregon. That education has nothing to do with the needs of our communities here ... How are we supposed to build a sense of belonging with our kids when their

education tells them that success looks like somebody else, is somewhere else, doing something else?

In Alaska, the state legislature has directed that $18 million be used to improve education systems after it was sued for inequity in rural schools. As a teacher, you can try to join two projects through the Coalition for Education Equity. The Educator Quality and Quantity project is attempting to increase the number of Alaska's teachers and administrators, improve teacher preparation, and increase teacher retention. The Ed Connector program wants to expand school district administration and increase leadership collaboration.

Despite improvements, American Indian students struggle with attendance and discipline. American Indian students represent about 0.6 percent of all students, but they account for 2 percent of the students expelled, represent 5 percent of students restrained or placed in seclusion, and are 1.9 times more likely to be chronically absent than White elementary school students.

What Can You Do to Counter Indigenous Stereotypes?

Engage without appropriating. Learn the traditions and the sources so you can pass the information forward appropriately. Expand the reach of American Indian history so it is more than Thanksgiving or a chapter in history class.

When teaching about feminism, teach about tribes like the Haudenosaunee, which has always been matrilineal and has matriarchal clans.

Kukahiko left me with this wise idea: "You can't change the system by treating the symptoms. You have to treat the conditions that are creating the problems in the first place."

Name the Original Inhabitants

Share information about the native inhabitants in your area with your students. You can start with a Google search focused on tribes in your location. Trace back the history to find tribal names.

I live near Cleveland, Ohio. A quick search of several reputable websites revealed that Ohio tribes included the Shawnee, Ottawa, Seneca, Wyandot, Miami, Delaware, Eel River Indian, Munsee, Chippewa, Piankashaw, Sauk, Potawatomi, Wea, Kaskaskia, and Iroquois, among others. However, there was a strange occurrence in Northeast Ohio that left the Cuyahoga Valley nearly empty for about one hundred years. Between 1000 and 1600, an unnamed tribe of American Indians lived in the area and practiced Whittlesey culture. Little is known about the tribe or tribes that lived there because their presence was largely gone before White immigrants arrived in the area in the mid-1600s. Pottery and arrowheads were left at village sites.

At first, historians thought the tribes left due to the "Beaver Wars," which were conflicts with White immigrants over who would prevail in the beaver pelt trades. However, a new theory suggests that disease from White immigrants spread so rapidly between American Indian populations that the tribes were wiped out before the first White immigrants settled in the area.

By the late 1700s, some tribes had returned to the area, like the Delaware and Seneca-Cayuga. Most of these tribes were Iroquoian speaking and were an amalgamation of other displaced tribes. Within one lifetime, most American Indians were forced to leave the area. They had lost their lands due to encroachment and violence from White immigrants despite the Treaty of Greeneville in 1795, which said White immigrants could not settle in northern Ohio. Some American Indians moved into western Ohio and took up residence there. Others took a final stand during the War of 1812 but ultimately lost.

In your research, select one or two tribes. Find their modern-day relatives at the primary source. For example, because many of the tribes in the area of modern-day Ohio were under the influence of the Iroquois, facts about culture can be derived from there. The Iroquois Nation is now known as the Onondaga Nation, and its website has a whole section on the culture, including their value of giving thanks.

For elementary students, start teaching about the Indigenous people in your area and their customs, past and present. If students ask what happened to them, have the knowledge to explain how or why their tribe was removed and where they went. If you don't know, admit it and tell them you'll find out. Then do your best to follow up.

Many tribal nations would be happy to hear from a teacher who wants to get the information right. Remember that you're focusing on who these people are from their perspective, not through the lens of White immigrants.

Define Success

Kaʻanohiokalā Kalama-Macomber is the education specialist for Nā Hopena Aʻo. She said that OHE has a vision of "When we do Hawaii, everyone succeeds."

The idea of success should be different for each classroom. There is no one-size-fits-all prescription or objective grading system. Already, schools across the country are moving away from SAT/ACT scoring and AP weighting systems as a way to "objectively" judge students.

This is where a curriculum that is specific to your geographic location and demographic community is important. Specific grading rubrics like in Chapter 8 may be helpful.

Work with your class to ask what success looks like for them. This can be done as a group activity. Have your students define success in the classroom.

Is success being a good friend, and what does that mean? Is success working together or working quietly? Does success change depending on the activity? What does it mean to be successful in their family and their community?

This definition of success can be extrapolated throughout the year. When teaching, ask or direct students as to how this lesson can apply in the community. I remember learning about percentages when I was an elementary school student. I did not care until my teacher told me that I needed to know percentages because it would help me figure out how much candy I could buy at a store. She explained that there was a thing called sales tax, and even if I counted up the price for all the candy I wanted, I still needed to get a percentage of the total to add to the cost. I still think about that today when I get to the register.

Kukahiko said it best. He explained that we want to "really transition our students from knowledge consumers to knowledge producers."

Chapter 5

LATINO

Latino culture isn't homogenous, and one person cannot speak for the whole race. Latino heritage and cultures come from a mix of nations in Central and South America as well as North America and some Caribbean Islands. It also is heavily influenced by Spain's colonization. In fact, Latino isn't the only term used to describe this race or ethnicity.

Latinx is a gender-neutral term used instead of Latino/Latina. Latino/a is a term used to describe people who come from Latin America, including those from non-Spanish-speaking countries like Haiti and Brazil. Hispanic is a term used to describe people who speak Spanish or come from Spanish descendants, and it includes people from Spain. While it may be more politically correct to use Latinx, many Latinos still use Hispanic, Latino/a, or their individual nationality. In this section, Hispanic and Latino will be used interchangeably.

Emily Key, the director of education at the Smithsonian's Latino Center, helped me define these terms. She told me not to get too stuck on the labels and to think of my audience. Who will know the term "Latinx" and who will know the term "Latino"?

Key remarked, "One of the things that we are trying to do with the Molina Gallery is explain the labels but also get past the labels. Most people in the community do not use Hispanic or Latino outside of things like documents for demographics.

If you're speaking colloquially on a day-to-day basis, they usually identify with their country of heritage."

The Molina Family Latino Gallery aims to present bilingual stories of Latino history and contributions to the US. Its opening at the National Museum of American History was delayed due to COVID-19 and is now set for 2022.

The Stereotypes

Illegal Immigrants

There is this strange idea that people coming to the US can somehow lose their personhood and become "illegals" just because of the way they try to immigrate. This "illegal" stereotype is widely used to describe Latino people, despite the fact that many Latino people have roots in the US.

Central and South Americans used to be fully native people before Europeans arrived. Their territories stretched into the US before there were these artificial borders. Like Indigenous people, many Latinos are not immigrants. Their grandparents and great-grandparents have history in this country; this was their country.

After Europeans arrived, Spain primarily colonized Central and South America. England and France colonized North America. Colonization, though, is not a kind of cultural exchange. In most cases, native cultures and languages were suppressed by law or by force. Native people were killed or forcibly removed from their lands. Mayans and Aztecs were enslaved by the Spanish during war. Strong nations became weak and could not defend themselves due to the sicknesses brought by Europeans.

In Central and South America, Spanish culture reigned supreme to the detriment of native language, culture, and religion. That's why the primary language in these areas is still Spanish.

There is this generalization that Latino people crossed the river from Mexico or came over on rafts from Cuba. During the Trump presidency, there was toxic rhetoric about building a wall to stop illegal immigration and the type of people who immigrate to the US from our southern border. His statements and these ideas are frighteningly and statistically incorrect. According to a Pew Hispanic Center report, four out of five Latinos—including virtually all Puerto Ricans— are US citizens.

> Did you know Puerto Rico is a US territory? Puerto Ricans are US citizens. Think of it this way: if you can travel there without a passport, then the people who live there are US citizens too.

Between 2010 and 2020, the US population grew by 22.7 million and over half of that population was made up of Hispanic people, many of whom identified as multiracial. This increase includes 9.3 million Hispanic newborn babies who were born here. Immigration, legal and otherwise, is also trending down for the Hispanic population.

For information on the Deferred Action for Childhood Arrivals (DACA) policy and the Development, Relief, and Education for Alien Minors (DREAM) Act, skip to Chapter 7. Note that if your student is otherwise safe at home, do not pry into their citizenship status.

So why aren't Latinos counted as Indigenous people? Well, they are. Kind of. Native people and Spanish immigrants had children together—sometimes consensually, sometimes native women were raped. Native people had children with Black people, who also had been brought over as slaves. This intermingling has led to the diversity that is included in Latino.

The only law that defines who is Latino and who is not was written in the 1970s, and it describes this as "Americans who identify themselves as being of Spanish-speaking background and trace their origin or descent from Mexico, Puerto Rico, Cuba, Central and South America, and other Spanish-speaking countries."

The Pew Research Center defines Hispanic as follows: "Anyone who says they are. And nobody who says they aren't."

Tacos, Trumpets, and Sombreros

Latino people—like other minorities—are at risk of being stereotyped into the Four Fs, as described by Edward Hall in his 1976 book *Beyond Culture*. The Four Fs are flags, food, festivals, and fashion, or what is known as visible culture. According to some texts, there can even be Five Fs, with the fifth being famous people.

Use the Four Fs as a starting point but never an ending point when learning about someone's culture. Find what is described as the "deep culture," which includes values and beliefs.

Beyond the Fs

Make a table like the one below for any Latin American country, and fill it in with the Four Fs with your students. This activity can be applied to countries and cultures outside of Latin America as well.

Visible Culture	Expanded Meaning	Deep Culture
Flag	What do the colors or symbols mean?	What does the flag mean today? How are the original meanings of the flag reflected today?
Food	What is the food made of?	How has the food changed since colonization or coming to the US? How is it significant to its people?
Festival	What does the festival celebrate?	How is this festival similar or different to festivals in the US? Why is this festival important to the culture?
Fashion	Who wore it? What was it made of?	Is this clothing still used? What is it used for? How has fashion changed?

If you want to add a famous person, the "Expanded Meaning" column would contain what the person is known for. The "Deep Culture" column would list the contributions they have made in their home country or in the US. An example would be Honduran American America Ferrera, an actress turned philanthropist and activist. Two examples of the chart appear below.

Mexico

Visible Culture	Expanded Meaning	Deep Culture
Mexican flag	The colors relate to the fight for independence, Catholicism, and the Spaniards who fought for freedom.	Catholicism and colonization have deeply shaped the values of Mexican Americans. Community is a central component, and there is a focus on collectivism rather than independence.
Tacos	Tacos used to be made with soft corn tortillas and fish. Tacos were infused with American staples like cheese in the 1920s. The crunchy shell didn't happen until the 1940s.	Tacos predated the arrival of the Spanish, and they were even documented as a first feast enjoyed by Europeans. Taco Bell is not Mexican food and doesn't serve what's considered real tacos.
Dia de los Muertos	This holiday is celebrated on the first days of November to remember loved ones who have passed on.	The idea of someone being dead or a ghost is not seen as scary. There is great importance placed on family and ancestors.

Visible Culture	Expanded Meaning	Deep Culture
Sombreros	These wide-brimmed hats cast a shadow over the neck and shoulders. They were designed to keep the heat of the environment off people.	The hats started with mestizo cowboys in Central Mexico. Sombreros are now also worn by mariachi players. The name sombrero comes from the Spanish/ Spain word for hat. Other cultures, like Texas cowboys and Filipinos, also have wide-brimmed hats or have adopted the sombrero into their own style.

El Salvador

Visible Culture	Expanded Meaning	Deep Culture
Flag of El Salvador	Blue represents the skies of the country and both oceans that surround Central America.	Native American cultures cultivated the indigo plant, which is used to produce blue dye. The dye was then monetized and used by the Spanish who called it "the blue gold" until coffee dominated the economy.
Pupusas	These are thick flatbread made with cornmeal and stuffed with a variety of ingredients. This is the national dish, and there is even a day when it is celebrated.	It is believed that the native Pipil tribes made pupusas. They were initially half-moon shaped and vegetarian. After the Spanish arrived, meats were included. After the Salvadoran civil war in the 1980s, immigrants brought pupusas to other countries and they started to spread.

Visible Culture	Expanded Meaning	Deep Culture
Indepen-dence Day	El Salvador's National Day is September 15, and it celebrates the independence of Central American provinces from Spain in 1821.	As in the US, student bands participate in parades on Independence Day. El Salvador also fought for its independence from a European power, Spain, alongside other Central American provinces. Cars fly flags of these Central American provinces, including Costa Rica, El Salvador, Guatemala, Honduras, and Nicaragua. September 15 is the day that the Act of Independence of Central America was composed, which is similar to the Declaration of Independence.
Huipil	This is a blouse worn by Indigenous women and girls, and it is often embroidered. Usually, it is made of woven cotton or wool.	The dominant native group of El Salvador was called Pipil, and they spoke Nawat. Many times a huipil is worn with a long skirt. Now a huipil is worn for traditional purposes or ceremonies.

The next time there is a classroom celebration or festival of cultures, experience it and then dig deeper. Taste the food, learn about where it came from, and then ask your students questions. You can assign them to take those questions and answers back home, and dig into some history. Or you can do that yourself and share it with the class.

Think about Religion

Catholic missionaries were sent to convert people from their native beliefs. Central and South Americans gained their own saints and customs, mixing them with native rituals. While Catholicism is on the decline with Latino people in the US, the culture is still part of their history. Catholic social teaching emphasizes such things as a call to family and community. How might this impact the values of your students? Let's say an issue comes up for which they have to choose between schoolwork or helping out their family. What might they choose? It isn't wrong if they choose to help their family first. It is just different.

How might this change their behavior in the classroom? Your Latino student sees a fellow student that needs help. They get out of their seat without permission and cross the classroom to help that student. They are focused first on their friend instead of classroom rules. How can you handle this in a way that is still respectful of their culture?

Gangs/Drug Lords

There is this idea that all Latino people are in gangs or their parents/siblings belong to gangs, especially if they live in a major city. This is not true, and it plays into harmful gender and sexuality stereotypes, such as a tendency toward violence and toxic masculinity. Boys are supposed to be interested in cars or motorcycles. Boys are supposed to be macho and want tattoos.

This is especially problematic when the stereotype intersects with Latino men or boys that belong to the LGBTQ community. These boys can be bullied and beaten until they start to perform the same toxic stereotypes.

In elementary school classrooms, young Latino boys should be allowed to express themselves the same way as any other boy or girl. In pre-K, boys should be able to pretend to be stay-at-home dads and play house. If they want to wear pink in third grade, they should feel confident with their choice. If they want to pick a sticker of a heart instead of a truck, that is their prerogative. Don't let someone pick on them for their preferences.

Other Barriers to Education That Latino People Face

Lack of Representation

When you evaluated your classroom in Chapter 1, you probably realized that very little literature features Latino students as the main characters. This is not an anomaly. While Latino people are a large part of the population growth, they are still underrepresented. Children's book illustrator David Huyck has created an infographic using data from the University of Wisconsin-Madison School of Education Cooperative Children's Book Center that details the main character's race in children's books by percentage. In 2018, only 5 percent were Latino, up from 2.4 percent in 2015.

In contrast, 50 percent of the main characters were White, 27 percent were animals or other nonhumans, 10 percent were Black, 7 percent were Asian or Pacific Islander, and 1 percent were Indigenous people. If children's books aligned more with the US Census results, Latino representation should be closer to 20 percent.

Key has worked with the Latino Center for over a decade, and some of her favorite resources are children's books. She advised, "Think about using children's books that are first-voice authors as a way to empower young people to see their communities whenever possible. It takes the story from something that happened to someone to something that could happen to you or that is related to you. The power for the non-person-of-color is that they actually see that people of color write books."

Key warned against using the same book year after year, especially if it involves animals. She recounted a time she spoke to a teacher who was teaching diversity with an old, award-winning book about animals: "A lot of times we go to the go-to book, and we don't change it because it's the one we know the best. In their mind, they didn't see a problem with teaching diversity by equating people of color to animals. It's not that they are OK with it. It's that they haven't even thought of it that way."

This is a frustrating trend. It's as if people who aren't White are othered in such a way that they need to be uplifted to animal status to be equal. There are whole studies and movements related to how people of color need to be seen as people. In 2018, activist and author Hannah Drake issued a challenge on her blog for people of color to "hold your space" when walking on the sidewalks and riding on the train, and not to generally shrink yourself so the White person can feel more comfortable. Anecdotal responses poured in, confirming that people of color are still expected to give way for White people. I know I do it all the time.

Take these anecdotes above and compare them to a 2010 study in the *Journal of Experimental Social Psychology* called "Empathy Constrained: Prejudice Predicts Reduced Mental Simulation of Actions during Observation of Outgroups," which found that White people showed less brain activity when watching a minority do a simple task than when they watched another White person do that same task. Some even showed "as little activity as when they watched a blank screen."

What does this study mean? It means that, generally, White people devalue people of color in everyday settings. People of color are invisible when they aren't disturbing the peace, and this falls in line with the pervasive erasure of culture and the oppression that colonialism brought with it. People of color were servants, not to be seen or heard. They are the ghosts that stock your shelves or pick your food. Are they really even there?

So, of course, you don't see me on the sidewalk. Of course, you don't move for me. I am not a person. I am just a small blip on your radar. I am the deer under the Amur tiger. I am the final stepping-stone at the summit of the mountain. Only when I fall will you see me.

I understand that many teachers can't just buy more books. When you do have the opportunity, though, look for ones with minority characters as the lead characters. While you wait, tell stories in which the Latino character is the main character. This could be as simple as changing the name of a character from John to Jose. Do not limit the Latino stories to stories of culture. While it is important for all students to learn about the heritage of different people, these "different people" are more than their heritage. They are also American, and they can tell American stories. Don't limit these narrators to the Four Fs. Did you know the equivalent name for Harold in Spanish is Haroldo? Perhaps Harold from *Harold and the Purple Crayon* could become Haroldo, a fair-skinned Latino kid with a purple crayon.

Outside of picture books, this issue of a lack of representation occurs in textbooks on American history, in classroom materials, and among professionals. How can you help students,

White and minority, see the accomplishments and history of Latino people in the US?

- Highlight successful Latino people across industries. See the "Examples of Notable BIPOC" chart in Chapter 10.

- Bring in successful Latino adults from the community or surrounding communities.

- Teach history concurrently. When kids learn about the states, remember to include Puerto Rico. When you teach about Halloween or fall festivals, include Dia de los Muertos. Check out materials on this subject online on the Smithsonian Latino Center's Teaching and Learning page. When kids learn about national monuments, include ones like the César E. Chávez National Monument and El Morro National Monument. When learning about health and how illnesses spread, include the Cuban epidemiologist and researcher Carlos Juan Finlay.

Being Underestimated

Teachers and administrators may assume Latino students are immigrants or that they don't speak English well. They are talked to slower as if they were young children. These students are quickly placed in lower-level or English as a second language (ESL) courses. This can take away from real education time and opportunities for higher-placement classes.

Their grades may suffer, not because they don't understand but because they are bored. Teachers and peers may assume they can't do better. Because of cultural differences, parents defer to the teacher's decision, and so it spirals into a self-fulfilling prophecy. If Latino students are placed in lower-level courses in primary school, they cannot reach their full potential in secondary school. Teachers and counselors do not recommend four-year universities. They are pigeonholed into trade positions.

To combat this, have high expectations. As with every other student, advocate for them and present challenging classwork. Encourage them and their parents to speak their mind.

Mark Lopez, the director of race and ethnicity research at the Pew Research Center, told me an interesting cultural fact. Latino people give deference to their elders and show respect for the people above them. Many times, in an education setting, this translates to not asking questions.

In our interview, Lopez remembered that he avoided going to his professors' office hours in graduate school even when he needed help, but he saw his White colleagues do the exact opposite. "I would go to the library and buckle down and figure it out. I didn't want the professor to know that I don't know, whereas my White colleagues would go talk to the professor," he recalled. "Then, when I became a professor, I saw it from the other side. I found that Latino students would toil and struggle off on their own and not take advantage that there was a Latino professor that wanted to help. The best thing is if your teachers and professors know who you are. That notion of respecting people of authority and not questioning gets in the way of some young Latinos' own needs to learn something."

This trait of not questioning extends to parents as well. Parents who do speak English, and who find the time to speak to the teacher outside of work, still may not communicate their concerns or questions when it comes to what action to take for their children or what classes they should go into.

"What I found in our surveys is that many Hispanic parents put a lot of faith in the schools to do the right thing for their children," revealed Lopez. "They give the schools a higher valuation than White parents do for the Whiter schools. The parents may not want to question the teacher, even though they may think [something is] the wrong thing to do. Maybe they don't want their child in a bilingual education program, but that is what the administrator and teacher recommends."

The best way to connect with parents is to build a relationship with them and build trust. Ask what they think and draw them out. This starts with making parent-teacher meetings work for them. Some parents are working two or three jobs. Some parents do not have readily available email access. Sometimes a parent may be late for a meeting they are able to get scheduled. Let it be OK.

While many Latino people speak English, there is still a lack of bilingual material in classrooms or for parents, which can make communication difficult. For more information on this, see Chapter 7.

Segregation and Lack of Access

In many places throughout the US, schools are still very much segregated. It's not just the Black kids or Latino students sitting together at lunch either. It's whole schools. Sometimes this is due to how the districts are drawn; methodical, racially motivated housing policies; or remnants of historic oppression. It still affects students today.

As of September 2021, President Joe Biden has created a new initiative to break down systemic barriers facing Latino students from early childhood through college. Twenty-one percent of Latino children were living in poverty in 2019, while the national average was 14 percent. New Mexico, the state with the largest population of Latino residents, lost a lawsuit that found that the state is not equally providing education to its students. The state has even taken federal money but reduced funding to the affected schools.

Even before the US Supreme Court case *Brown v. Board of Education,* Mexican Americans pushed for equality in schools. A good upper-level picture book called *Separate Is Never Equal* by Duncan Tonatiuh, shows how the Mendez family fought for desegregation in 1947. The problem is that segregation is still an issue for many races. How do you get to integration and equity when you're still fighting undercover segregation?

In the book *Overturning Brown: The Segregationist Legacy of the Modern School Choice Movement* by Steve Suitts, the author reveals some modern segregationist tactics, like how private schools select token students. "Frequently, White private schools have chosen Asian or Pacific Island children to break their completely segregated enrollment in order to reach a token level of diversity for an IRS tax exemption …. Only White students and students with Asian ancestries were in private schools in numbers that exceeded or generally match the representation in school-age population. In 42 states, the percentage of Asian students in private schools exceeded the state's percentage of school-age Asian children."

Attitudes and policies like this not only push ideas like the model minority myth but perpetuate stereotypes like lazy immigrants and dumb Black kids.

Fun Fact

Some Hispanic people identify more with their Spanish/Latino side than their Indigenous side. They still consider themselves Latino, but many times their ancestry is more from the Spaniard side. They identify more with Spanish culture than with Indigenous customs and beliefs. Others view it as more of an American Latino culture in the way that Black people and Africans view themselves separately.

I understand that you, as a teacher, have little control over the composition of your classroom. I am not going to ask experienced teachers to quit a job and go to segregated communities to teach.

The other side of this coin is that even in cases in which schools are desegregated, there is still an issue of a lack of access. The COVID-19 pandemic has highlighted this issue. Kids needed to be taught virtually, but not all households had Wi-Fi access, let alone a computer for each student. If they had the computer and the Wi-Fi, could one parent stay home to watch kids?

As said in Chapter 2, poor socioeconomic standing affects many students of color. Parents may work six days a week.

Let's say you assign a project, and the student needs to go to the local library for internet access. That student needs to find a responsible adult to take them to the library. Maybe their parents can only take them on Sunday when the library and buses have limited hours. How far does that child need to walk to complete the assignment? How many buses do they need to take? Do they need an ID or other information for them or their parents to get a library card?

The reality is, there isn't much you can do here. To reach out to segregated communities, you can film your instruction. You can post it to YouTube. But if these underserved students do not have an internet connection or do not know your curriculum exists, how will they get it? If they do not understand it, who can explain it to them?

You can eliminate homework or minimize it to time spent reading at home. You can make sure class work and projects can be completed during class time. You can talk to parents about free or discounted Wi-Fi programs. Mostly, just be aware of the possible limitations of your students, even if this means you literally walk their path.

When I was in middle school, I wanted to take shop class. My shop class was at one end of the school and my previous class (science class) was at the exact opposite end in a corner. In between shop class and science class was my locker. I had five minutes from the time the bell rang to round the corner, get to my locker, open the lock, throw in my heavy science book, and navigate to shop class. The late bell would always be ringing as the doors to the shop class came in sight.

The shop teacher, a tall White man, blamed me for hanging out with friends in the five minutes, and he would not allow me to be even a few seconds late. When I tried to explain that I was small and doing my best, this lanky adult man told me that he could walk from the science room to the shop room in under five minutes just fine. Never mind that he was a teacher with more than a foot on me. I am a little over five feet tall now. In middle school, I wasn't even that.

My parents finally stepped in and had a meeting with the man during which he literally had me put on my backpack and timed me with a stopwatch. He watched me walk as fast as I could with my short legs in an empty hallway after school. He stood behind me as I did the combination on my locker. He trailed me as I kept fast walking up to his classroom. When I was just reaching the doors at the five-minute mark again, my parents told him to imagine how much more of a struggle it is when the halls are crowded. Imagine the pressure I felt to get my locker combination right on the first try. Imagine what would happen if I needed to ask the science teacher a question at the end of class.

The shop teacher finally relented and let me be one minute late to class.

Walk the Path

Before you assign an out-of-school project, get on the bus on a Sunday to the nearest library. At the library, see if you can complete the work while the library is open. Can you find a free computer? Are there time limits on the computer? Do you need to check out any materials to take home? What are the limits for kids to check out materials? What information do you need for a library card? See if you can get back home before the parent chaperone would need to leave to catch the bus to make dinner.

Chapter 6

ASIAN

When we think about teaching with equity, it is easy to place our brains into Black versus White thinking, but US schools contain all kinds of students, and these minority populations are growing. It is equally important to examine cultural and race issues that are not on the Black and White line.

The Monolith

Did you know Asian American is a super broad term that encompasses a huge swath of land masses, each with their own cultures, stereotypes, and challenges?

Asian Americans are often thought of as coming from Japan, Korea, and China, but the term also includes people from Vietnam, Thailand, the Philippines, India, Pakistan, Pacific Island nations, and more. (It should be noted that Pacific Islander is an umbrella term itself for the many Melanesian, Micronesian, and Polynesian cultures and ethnicities.)

Andrea Kim Neighbors is the manager of education initiatives at the Smithsonian Asian Pacific American Center. Before she worked for the Smithsonian, Neighbors was a museum educator for Wing Luke Museum of the Asian Pacific American Experience in Seattle, Washington. She told me of a time when she was giving a tour to a diverse elementary school class. The class had arrived at a section of the tour that had images of businesses in Seattle's Japantown before World War II.

"We were talking about the signs and how vibrant the Japanese American community was before World War II. Some of the students got really excited because they were Japanese American, and they had heard stories from their grandparents about this time. They were seeing themselves represented," Neighbors recalled. "Then some of their classmates yelled at them and said, 'You're lying. You're not Japanese. You're Chinese.' I remember the teacher said nothing. The Japanese American students shrunk in their seats, and their whole demeanor changed. They looked so down. I pulled them to the side and thanked them for sharing and told them that they had very important roots here."

Neighbors reflected that she has seen the same thing many times in her life and on how it happened to her in elementary school. One time, she was in school, and she stated how she was mixed Korean and White. Other students told her she wasn't and labeled her as something else.

If this happens in your classroom, as a teacher, you need to stand up for that child and believe the primary source. If a student says, "I am Filipino," then that is what they are. It is their heritage and culture. It is distinct.

Check out the Smithsonian Asian Pacific American Center's website and its "We Are Not a Stereotype" video series that breaks down the monolithic stereotype of Asian Americans. These videos are made for teachers and educators to learn about Asian Americans.

The Model Minority Myth

This myth stereotypes Asian Americans as hardworking, quiet, smart, successful, and valuing education. Common stereotypes associated with the model minority myth include the following:

- Being prompt
- Keeping to themselves
- Studying hard
- Not making a fuss, especially about issues of racism or equality
- Being diligent
- Being hard workers
- High achieving in school
- Having pressure to be in medical professions

This model minority myth was created as a weapon to use against other people of color, and it does not encapsulate all Asian Americans. It also pushes stereotypes, even though they're positive, on a group of people that still has the same issues that other human beings have.

How Is the Model Minority Myth a Weapon?

When there is an idea that some immigrants and some minorities are successful, the upper-class majority can then point to other minorities and say, "See! It's possible to be successful as a minority in the US. [Insert race] just isn't trying hard enough."

It sows tension and discrimination between the races in the same way that the upper-class pits Black people and poor White people against one another. People believe Asian Americans are well off and do not need the help that other communities need. This idea is inaccurate and ignores the high poverty rates that Asian Americans can and do suffer from, the growing income inequality between Asian American groups, and the fewer resources that are allocated to their communities. Historically, East Asian Americans were the ones referred to in the model minority myth, and this ignores so many other communities.

Asian Americans also have their own barriers, like the "bamboo ceiling," which are processes that exclude Asian Americans from executive positions. Even though they may be invited into the boardroom or the corporate structure, it is difficult to rise to a position of leadership.

The reality is that there is no model minority. The term was coined by William Petersen in a 1966 article he wrote for the *New York Times*, titled "Success Story: Japanese American Style." He focused on Confucian values, the two-parent household, and the way Japanese Americans seemed to blossom out of internment camps at the end of World War II, but his article largely ignored the purposeful political and social changes that led to Asian Americans appearing successful. The year before Peterson wrote that article, the 1965 Immigration Act was passed, allowing a greater number of immigrants from Asia to enter the country, but these immigrants were limited to, mostly, professionals and scientists. Highly educated Asian immigrants and their children flooded the population, increasing outward average success, such as mean household income. The Asian American success story was popular with the press, and it was used to improve people's opinions about the community, which opened more avenues for Asian Americans in employment.

If you were a 1960s White man, whom would you employ? The smart, quiet Asian man or the lazy, loud Black man?

See how this oversimplified, stereotyped statement is divisive, untrue, and harmful?

How Are Positive Stereotypes Bad in the Classroom?

Asian students can often be overlooked. Teachers assume that because the student is quiet and Asian, they understand the content. They assume that the student is naturally gifted and do not notice the extra studying the child puts in. Teachers assume the parents are like "tiger moms" and are involved in the child's schoolwork and grades.

What if the student needs extra help but isn't asking and no one is noticing? What if the student isn't naturally gifted and is working many extra hours to be where their peers are? This can lead to burnout or the student's feeling like they are choking under pressure. Students can feel depersonalized, as if they are not expected to be any more than their race.

On the flip side, some teachers will assume Asian students do not speak English. These teachers will speak slowly to the students even when English is their first language. The student then may not speak up because they don't want to be put on the spot.

How Can I Fix This?

Like anyone else, treat everyone like an individual. Check in on your quiet students and read body language. Think about these questions:

● Are they clenching their pencil?

● Are they studying during free time or play time?

- How do they look when they get their test scores? Are they happy or apathetic?

- Have you met and spoken to the parents?

- What does the student like that isn't academically related?

- What does the student want to be when they grow up? Does this career stem from an expectation or something they are actually interested in?

The Negative Stereotypes

Asian Americans face the struggle of feeling like perpetual foreigners even after generations being born and living in the US. Some of the feeling stems from microaggressions about their appearance, ancestry, or lack of an accent. Other stereotypes are said straight to their faces, like "jokes" about war brides or mail-order brides.

Asian women especially are cast as subservient or conservative. They supposedly listen to their men, and they cook and clean without fuss. They do not talk back, and they are always thin and small. They are here to serve. As cited in Chapter 2, this puts them at risk for violence when they do speak out or break the mold.

Another stereotype is that Asian women who marry Asian men of their same ethnicity did so because of an arranged marriage. While matchmaking does still occasionally happen, it is set up after the adult son or daughter consents to trying it out. Many times, it is the same thing as a White parent saying to their child, "You know my friend Mary has a son who just graduated too. You should go out sometime."

With the COVID-19 pandemic, the idea of Yellow Peril or Asian American and Pacific Islander (AAPI) Hate has resurfaced again. Yellow Peril is a type of scapegoating that plays to White people's fears about Asians, like the spread of communism or Buddhism. In the past, Asian people were lynched because of those fears. Today, it is the idea that Asian people have diseases. News channels were reporting on elderly Asian Americans being pushed or and beaten in 2020, and these problems persist. Rhetoric around the virus became inflammatory because of President Trump's dog whistles about the "Chinese virus" and his anti-Asian sentiments.

Dusky Peril, an offshoot of Yellow Peril, is based on fear of Hindu and Sikh people coming to America, especially to the West Coast, like California. Today, Sikh often get mistaken for Muslim people, and there are anti-Muslim sentiments that came after the September 11 attacks. Unfortunately, this attitude was reignited by President Trump's Muslim ban, the fearmongering toward refugees from Syria, and the sudden, recent withdrawal from Afghanistan.

South Asians have also been called Arab or Middle Eastern. This is not a "recognized race" when it comes to checking boxes on government forms though, so in this book, South Asian is under the Asian American umbrella.

Right now, many South Asian students and their families suffer from Islamophobia even if Islam is not their religion. Students are often stereotyped as terrorists because of their skin color or clothing. Classmates will make jokes about bombs in turbans or mock girls for wearing hijabs. Even worse, some students have tried to "liberate" girls in their class by pulling off their head coverings.

Though many South Asians immigrated to the US after 2000, some arrived in the 1800s on the West Coast. That hasn't stopped cyberbullying and students being told to "go back to their own country." In elementary school, this trend seems to crop up in the later years.

Teaching religion in elementary school can be tricky, but you can teach without teaching. Explain that Islam can be simplified by introducing it as a sequel. Talk to your students about their favorite book or movie series. Then you can say, "Did you know religion can be like that? Judaism is the first book in a series. Christianity is the sequel. Islam is the final book in the series. Each book has its own name: the Torah, the Bible, the Qur'an. Some people like the first book, others like the second, and still others like the third."

How to Promote Equity for Asian American Students in the Classroom

Sometimes trying to find out how to be equitable can feel insurmountable. Here are some simple things you can do to promote equity for Asian American students:

- Learn about the individuals in your class. Encourage—but do not force—them to share when you talk about weekends or holidays or seasonal breaks.

- Ask about tangible things, like their favorite snack. Why is that their favorite?

  » If the snack is not something you've heard of, look it up. Chances are an Asian market in the nearest major city stocks it. You can try it on your own time and later talk to the student about your experience. If your school allows it, you can have days when you bring in students' favorite snacks to share.

- Share their stories with permission. Some students may be more willing to write down what they did on their holidays than tell the class out loud. Take the child aside and ask if you can share their stories later. Ask if they would like to be named or not. If they do not want to be named but are willing to share the story, you can share the story and say it came from someone in last year's class or someone you know. It may feel odd to tell a small lie, but many classes only have one or two Asian students. It quickly becomes very easy to figure out whose story it was.

- Learn each student's name. Many times, Asian American students with Asian-sounding names choose English names to make it easier for teachers and peers. If a student is willing to help you learn to pronounce their given name, then learn it and try until you get it. You can take time to practice it at home. A quick Google search will provide you with videos and audio clips of almost every ethnic name. If the student still wants you to use their English name, then use that.

- Learn about their customs. This requires work on your part to learn about what specific part of Asia your students, their relatives, or their ancestors came from. What holidays should you be mindful of? What customs or cultural practices might they follow? Remember that not every Japanese American student will be Shinto or Buddhist. Not every Chinese American student will care about receiving red envelopes on Lunar New Year or taking off their shoes at home. As you learn about the intricacies that make up your current and future students, you can learn about who they are and where their Asian heritage meets their US lives.

- Explain religious differences through unity. Learn the differences between Hinduism, Sikhism, and Islam so you can correct students if needed. Find common ground like how religions teach people to be good. You can also explain how people show their religion in different ways. Some Christians go to church every Sunday, some don't. Some Sikhs wear turbans. Others don't. Some Jewish people keep kosher, some don't.

What If Students or Parents Are Private and Do Not Want to Share?

Some Asian American students and parents may find it hard to share about things they feel they are not supposed to talk about. Viet Thanh Nguyen is a Pulitzer Prize-winning Vietnamese American novelist and professor. In a YouTube video called "In Conversation with Viet Thanh Nguyen," he speaks about how children of Vietnamese refugees were instructed by their parents not to speak about how they feel the US betrayed them during the Vietnam War.

He said, "The US came in, helped instigate this war, told the Vietnamese people, 'We will always be there for you. We'll fight for you. We'll never let you get taken over by the communists,' and then the US left .... [Vietnamese people] will only say this in Vietnamese because they feel they have to perform gratitude to America as a whole for rescuing them from communism."

Some Asian Americans feel that their lives and histories are private and personal. While talking with Neighbors about her own experiences, she said, "We [might] learn about our histories privately at home and in our communities. War might be a thing that a lot of us have in common. War devastated the Korean peninsula. War devastated China, Southeast Asia, and the Pacific Islands. American expansion and the atrocities of the Japanese military during World War II and before are something a lot of us have in connection to each other." She explained further, "War is not everyone's story, but it is connected to my story. There's a phrase I think about a lot: 'I'm here because you were there.' My father was in the military, and my mother was born right after the Korean War. They probably wouldn't have met if there was no military there."

Rochelle Hoi-Yiu Kwan is an oral history educator and a woman of many hats who has collaborated with the Smithsonian Asian Pacific American Center and works as a DJ called YiuYiu. Kwan and I talked about how it may not be that Asian Americans don't want to tell their stories. It may be about the approach. When she started working as a national facilitator with StoryCorps—a nonprofit organization that records stories from people all across the US and archives them in the Library of Congress American Folklife Center—she found there was a lack of Asian Americans coming in to tell their stories.

"As I was watching the way StoryCorps was trying to recruit people to do these interviews, I was thinking about my family. If someone came up to my family and was like, 'Hey, we want to record your story and put it into the Library of Congress. You can talk about anything you want,' I know that my family would never say yes to that." Kwan elaborated, "It wasn't that Asian Americans didn't want to tell their stories. It was our approach that wasn't culturally competent. It wasn't acknowledging the traumas that come from being immigrants, like coming from a country where the government recording information about you could be dangerous, or [dealing with] a language divide."

Kwan expanded StoryCorps's oral history process beyond doing interviews and started to build relationships with different Asian folks in New York City and around the country. She focused on creating workshops that got people thinking about how to have these conversations and why they should tell these stories. Then, in the workshops, the group talked about where the stories told would go and why it was important to archive them. At the end, the team would bring the recorded stories back to the community with listening parties so everyone could hear their own stories.

Kwan has continued to do this community-centered oral history work after parting with StoryCorps. She works with Think!Chinatown, produces on the podcast Self Evident, and consults with the Hunter College Asian American Studies Program.

Kwan described how sometimes the big talk, the immigration talk, can seem too big to tackle at first. Sometimes you need to pick one small thing to talk about, like someone's day or a relatable item, and eventually it naturally builds into the big talk. She described eloquently how this might "pull threads into memories."

She shared, "When I started inheriting these records and started to dig into music, I would call my dad every week and tell him about all the new stuff I was finding. Then he started telling me these stories he associated the different songs with, and then the disco parties he and his friends would do, then how he learned English through music. And then his immigration story."

The activities below can help you to introduce the subject and bring the context to students who are not Asian American.

Find the Memory

Think!Chinatown, a nonprofit organization based in New York City's Chinatown neighborhood, has a project called Everyday Chinatown. The project features a series of videos in which oral historians showcase household objects specific to the Chinese population. They ask different people what the object is, and many times the people willingly tell a story or memory from that story. Each video alternates between a story in English, Cantonese, and Mandarin Chinese. The videos are short and appropriate even for elementary schoolers.

Show an Everyday Chinatown video from Think! Chinatown. Discuss the objects in the videos. Reflect on everyday objects in your home and your students' homes that may tell stories. Encourage students to pick an object and ask their parents about that object. The student can take a photo of the object and then bring the oral history with the photo back to class.

For example, in my home, there is a map on the wall with my family's initials over different parts. That map has been there since before my children were born. That map tells everyone where we have traveled in the world, but it also reminds me of the past; how Black people used to not be able to travel freely because there were White-only or sundown towns. Sundown towns are towns where people of color are not welcome after dark. Sometimes it is just unpleasantness or an inability to rent a motel. Other times it results in violence. It reminds me of *The Negro Motorist Green Book*, which told Black people what places were safe to stay or eat or stop when traveling. It reminds me of how my freed ancestors moved from the South to West Virginia for mining jobs, how my father moved from West Virginia to Maryland to find a better life with a union job at the telephone company. The map reminds me of all the places I've been to, the places I want to go, and the places I want my kids to go because they can now.

The Love Languages

In my talk with Kwan, she spoke about growing up in a culture that focused on subtlety and showing without telling. "A lot of what [my parents] taught me about being Asian American was shown to me and not talked about. One of the things that is really big in the Asian diaspora, particularly for children of immigrants, is that parents don't say 'I love you' ever. But if they cut you a bowl of fruit and put it down next to you, that is them saying they love you."

In your classroom, lead with patience. Every child is different, and every child may ask for help differently. The popular book *The Five Love Languages* by Gary Chapman has a version for learning about children. The love languages are acts of service, words of affirmation, quality time, receiving gifts, and physical touch. You can assign parents to help their child take an online quiz to see what their love language is if the child is between nine and twelve. Explain to parents that it will be useful in telling you how to best instruct and interact with their kid. The quiz can be found at 5lovelanguages.com.

If parents do not have time or internet access, you can do the tests while at school. If the child is younger than eight, the website has some exercises to try to determine what the child's love language is.

If a child's love language is words of affirmation, they will probably do well when they are praised for their work or innovative thinking. If a child's love language is quality time, that student may excel when a teacher or a friend spends some extra one-on-one time helping them out with a problem. If a child's love language is acts of service, they may feel appreciated when someone helps tie their shoes or carry their books.

Students can share with one another what their love languages are so they can help build a cohesive classroom that focuses on respect. It also helps students with their interpersonal skills and their understanding that people are different. What works for someone might not mean the same thing to someone else.

Share Our Sayings

As for kids from many cultures, Asian American children can find it helpful if instruction comes in metaphors. This is an indirect way of speaking that tells a story and teaches a lesson. A common Filipino saying is "A broom is sturdy because its strands are tightly bound." It means that cooperation gets a job done quickly.

What sayings are in your classroom? List all the ones the kids know, such as "Don't cry over spilled milk." Then include sayings from across cultures. Let the kids try to figure out what they mean, and assist if necessary.

Saying	Meaning
Don't cry over spilled milk. (British)	What is done is done.
Teach a man to fish. (Chinese)	Teaching someone a life skill is better than doing it for them.
Dig the well before you're thirsty. (Chinese)	Plan ahead.
Even monkeys fall from trees. (Japanese)	Everyone makes mistakes even at things they are good at.
One hand can't hold two watermelons. (Persian)	You can't do everything.
A day of traveling will bring a basket full of learning. (Vietnamese)	To think outside the box, you have to leave your comfort zone.

How Do You Teach Asian American History?

The Smithsonian Asian Pacific American Center has a section called Learning Together for teachers to use in the classroom. This section includes activities and lesson plans on Asian American and Pacific Islander history, on anti-racism, and on making art and global connections.

Neighbors is particularly excited about the Making Art and Global Interconnections module. She said, "This is a series I loved working on because it broadens who is Asian American or Pacific Islander. It was created in partnership with artists and educators who didn't know each other before this project, and we found these interesting points of commonality to create a lesson plan that can be scaled up or down that lets the artists and art historian's perspective into the classroom."

The Learning Together section also has lists of books written by Asian Americans that can be used in the classroom. As expected as part of the Smithsonian, the Asian Pacific American Center's content is incredible, is free, and continues to grow.

Chapter 7

BILINGUAL AND IMMIGRANT

This chapter takes on the overlapping and challenging world of kids who speak multiple languages and/or are immigrant students. Asian American, Latino, Black, and certain Indigenous students may learn another language before or at the same time that they learn English. This chapter includes mixed languages like Hawaiian Pidgin.

The chapter refers to actual bilingual or immigrant students. It is important to make sure you do not automatically assume minority students are not English speakers. A common sentiment among minority students is the feeling of being treated as foreign in their own country, and part of this stems from comments about how well they speak English.

The Stereotypes

Immigrants Are Illegal Aliens from Mexico

There is an idea that immigrants come to the country illegally, which is mostly untrue.

Nearly forty million immigrants currently live in the US, and nearly thirty million of these people entered the country legally.

For those that do enter the country improperly, the Pew Research Center distinguishes immigrant status by unauthorized or undocumented immigrants instead of "illegal immigrants" or the inhuman title "illegal aliens." So I will be using the Pew Research Center term.

These unauthorized immigrants are usually stereotyped as being from Mexico or Central America. They are called all sorts of names, and there was even this strange idea that cropped up in the last decade that a wall could stop people from crossing the border.

Most unauthorized immigrants are not from Mexico. According to an April 2021 report from the Pew Research Center, "As of 2017, 4.9 million unauthorized immigrants in the US were born in Mexico, while 5.5 million were from other countries." Many of these "other countries" are in Asia.

The truth is, there used to be 12.2 million unauthorized immigrants in 2007, and that number went down to 10.5 million in 2017. Most of these unauthorized immigrants are not new to the country, with two-thirds having lived in the country for more than 10 years. Some arrived legally and just overstayed their visas. There has been a significant drop in new arrivals of unauthorized immigrants—before President Trump was elected. In 2021, there was an uptick of encounters at the southwest US border, but most of these ended up with expulsion before entry rather than apprehension once inside the US.

Unauthorized Immigrants Are Uneducated Laborers or Criminals

There has been a steady uptick in the number of unauthorized immigrants who have graduated from high school and college, according to reports by the Pew Research Center. Some come to this country with degrees. Others earn their degrees through policies and acts that support young children.

The Deferred Action for Childhood Arrivals, or DACA, is a US immigration policy that defers the deportation of children who entered the country unlawfully. It is renewable every two years, and eventually these people are eligible for a work permit. People who have committed felonies and/or serious misdemeanors are not eligible for the policy. This policy is also not a pathway for citizenship.

The Development, Relief, and Education for Alien Minors Act, or DREAM Act, grants temporary residency with the right to work to undocumented immigrants who entered the US as children. If these children later qualify, they can become permanent residents. These kids are known as Dreamers.

Immigrants/Bilingual Students Don't Speak English

Many immigrants speak English to some degree. Parents may have an accent, but they know enough to get their groceries and work a job. Children are even luckier. Their brains still have elasticity, and the best time to learn a second language is in early childhood, the earlier the better. So even if your students aren't fluent in English yet, they probably will be.

Did you know the high school dropout rate among Latino people dropped so low by 2014 that it helped lower the national dropout rate? Recent studies from the Pew Research Center found that even around 33 percent of unauthorized immigrants speak English proficiently. This means these parents and students know two languages! Usually, you have to put a child in private school to have them learn two languages at such a young age.

The Barriers to Equity

Along with common barriers to success and barriers that specifically relate to their race, immigrants and bilingual students have added challenges.

The Approach to Education

Like any other family, immigrant families can put intense pressure on students to succeed because these parents have provided their children with an opportunity and have sacrificed their native lands or homes or families to make a life here. They may seek out every opportunity for their children and overwhelm them with extracurricular activities and tutoring.

On the flip side, the student could have an almost complete lack of support. The parents may be too busy at work to help with homework. Because of the move or language barrier, the parents may not know what help is accessible to them or their students. The parents may not know all the possibilities for education after high school. They may not understand how gifted or honors classes work, or the importance of grades.

Introduce all your students to the opportunities at your school, and use a visual worksheet that can be taken home to show the educational structure in the US. You can check out a sample diagram on the National Center for Education Statistics website at https://nces.ed.gov/programs/digest/d01/fig1.asp. Go over the opportunities for advanced or alternative classes that students can take advantage of in elementary and secondary school. Show on the visual worksheet which kind of job requires what kind of education.

It is hard to know what is possible and how to reach those possibilities without guidance. Mark Lopez from the Pew Research Center said the best way to help students succeed is "knowing somebody that has gone through the system and knows how it works. Many Latinos might be the first in their family going to college."

Your students are at the elementary school level. They do not need to know the intricacies of scholarships, grants, and other financial aid yet. They do not need to know about standardized tests. These things can be mentioned and information can be sent home with parents.

ESL Classes

Speaking of alternate classes, some students are pulled out of classes to take ESL courses. While these classes can be helpful, some students and parents worry that they will miss valuable instruction time. These students may not have the time to review what they missed or have someone available to explain it to them at home. Students in these classes also miss out on making connections with their peers.

On the flip side, it has not worked to speak only English in the classroom and attend courses only in English. California tried that for 20 years, and after many lawsuits, it was repealed in 2016. The state has now started investing in bilingual education. A 2018 initiative called Global California 2030 is attempting to have half of all K–12 students participate in programs to become proficient in two or more languages by 2030. The ultimate goal is biliteracy for 75 percent of students by 2040. The California State Board of Education also approved the California English Learner Roadmap to better support English learners.

How to best serve your students remains to be seen. You're one teacher in a sea of 20 to 30 students. You can't provide one-on-one instruction if you wanted to. If your immigrant or bilingual students go to ESL classes, try to meet with them when they come back and let them know what they missed. If you can offer hours after school, offer them. If you know of a program that might help outside of school, bring it up to parents.

The Translator

Young bilingual students often become the unofficial translator for their parents and older family members. While this may expand the child's vocabulary, it also increases the stress on the child's mental health. Many times they are placed in situations in which they have to learn about family finances, personal or health information, and other adult conversations. They may end up missing homework because they are helping their parents fill out forms. Be mindful of this possibility.

Emily Key, from the Smithsonian's Latino Center, spoke with me about how these barriers actually stem from a lack of access. "We don't think about it, but that's a lack of access to their own time. This student may be calling the water company while their counterpart might have time to go to the library. There are these quiet barriers that you're not aware exist unless you're looking for them," she said.

A few years ago, comedian Cristela Alonzo posted this to Twitter: "Shout out to all immigrant kids that serve as translators for their parents, especially when you're a kid and have to try your best to translate words you don't know yet. I always hoped I guessed right." Alonzo then revealed how she translated everything from movies she watched together with her mother to information to help her mother find a diagnosis for her illness.

This one tweet set off a chain reaction of people sharing their experiences and the fears they had as children in adult situations. Some children had to balance checkbooks and read final notice papers. Others had to translate medical terms, talk to police during traffic stops, or translate the news on TV.

You may ask yourself, "What can I do? I'm not a translator. I don't know how to communicate."

If your school does not provide translators or important documents in different languages, request that they do. While you wait, try using Google Translate to help you communicate.

Make an effort to speak to the parents if no translator is available. Do not use the child as the translator. Type what you want to communicate with them. Find out the language they speak. Run your message through Google Translate. Email or text this message to them, and offer to show them how to do the same. It might not be perfect, but you are trying. Just like their response might not be perfect either.

For parent-teacher conferences, download the Google Translate app onto your phone and type in what you want to say. Have it play the translated audio out loud to the parent during the parent-teacher conferences.

Google Translate is your friend when creating or updating worksheets. Try to offer worksheets and handouts in English and the native language of your bilingual/immigrant students.

For math worksheets, avoid word problems if you can't translate them. If you can't avoid word problems, make sure the content makes sense for everyone and all the information is given. Do not assume every student knows there are nine innings in baseball.

For English coursework, encourage bilingual students to send you their files electronically in their own language when possible. Then run the assignments through Google Translate, and grade them based on content with a margin for error. If the students submit work in English and it is their second language, do not sink a grade because of spelling or punctuation. Yes, even punctuation is used differently in other countries.

Do not automatically give the bilingual or immigrant students the translated version of a worksheet. You can ask ahead of time if they would like one. If they do not, do not force them to take the translations. They may want to work on their English skills. If you see a student having trouble, especially if it is during a timed quiz, give that student a little more time to complete it. They may be translating the text from English to their native language, solving the question, and then translating the answer back from their native language to English.

If you're specifically looking for materials in Spanish, the Smithsonian's Latino Center website has bilingual materials on a variety of subjects, including inspirational Latino people, Latino holidays and history, and cultural expressions. Some of these include activities specifically for elementary students, like in the Resource Kit in the Learning Lab.

If your English-speaking students want to see translated material, let them see it and try to read it for themselves. Perhaps they will gain an interest in learning languages, perhaps they will gain empathy for the struggle of not knowing a language, perhaps they know some of the native language and can help you update language in the handout.

Travel in Your Own Classroom

Even if you do not teach a foreign language class or you do not have a student that speaks another language, try pretending to be foreign with your elementary students. Ask students if they've ever traveled somewhere where people do not speak English as the first language. Then introduce the idea that they are going to pretend to be in a classroom in another country. Some of the words they know will change. With upper elementary students, label commonly used items with their foreign language names and have students refer to it that way the whole day. For example, trash becomes basura (Spanish). Computer becomes computadora (Spanish).

For lower-level elementary students, use numbers. When you count, do it in the other language and use finger counting so they can visualize it. At the end of the day, ask students how difficult or easy it was to know the word for something but not really know it. Ask them to imagine how other kids their age feel when they come to this country and don't know the language.

Chapter 8

WORKSHEET EXAMPLES

Math

There are two big issues when it comes to equity with math word problems: a lack of representation through names and missing information. One solution to the first issue is to use the name tables in Chapter 10 to create these problems. Another solution is to use "you" and "I" to refer to the main characters in the word problem. A third option is to use titles or professions. If you choose the third option, use a variety of professions, including some that children may not already know. This exposes them to potential future careers and opens the door for later discussion.

The example below is a worksheet for the third-grade level when working on products using the 10s base. The Common Core standard is 3.NBT.3. The before and after versions show how easy changes can be.

Name: _____

Estimating Products

1. Mrs. Smith has 32 students in her class. If each student has 69 colored pencils, which expression shows how many colored pencils are in the classroom?

A. 30 x 70　　　　B. 40 x 70　　　　C. 30 x 60

2. George has 26 Spotify playlists. If each playlist is 48 minutes long, which expression shows how many minutes of music he has?

A. 20 x 50　　　　B. 30 x 50　　　　C. 20 x 60

3. Molly is a veterinarian. She treats 19 animals every day. Which expression shows the number of animals she has treated after 31 days?

A. 40 x 10　　　　B. 30 x 10　　　　C. 30 x 20

4. Larry's Lawn Company charges a customer $89 every month. Which expression shows how much money Larry makes after one year?

A. 90 x 10　　　　B. 90 x 20　　　　C. 80 x 10

5. John is a truck driver. He delivers 43 boxes to each destination he visits. If he visits 14 destinations every week, which expression shows how many boxes he delivers?

A. 50 x 10　　　　B. 40 x 20　　　　C. 40 x 10

6. Mr. Johnson is the librarian. He scans 57 items every 51 minutes. Which expression shows how many items he scans?

A. 60 x 50　　　　B. 50 x 50　　　　C. 60 x 60

7. Ella eats lunch 7 days every week. After 52 weeks, what is the expression that shows how many lunches she has eaten?

A. 10 x 60   B. 10 x 50   C. 0 x 50

8. Ms. White grades 15 tests every month. If she has 32 students, what is the expression that shows the number of tests she grades every month?

A. 10 x 30   B. 20 x 40   C. 20 x 30

9. Our school collected cans for recycling. We collected 64 bags with 88 cans inside each. What is the expression to find the total number of cans?

A. 60 x 90   B. 60 x 80   C. 70 x 90

10. A doctor takes care of 15 patients every day. After 66 days, what is the expression for the number of patients they have seen?

A. 10 x 70   B. 20 x 70   C. 10 x 60

After

Name: _____

Estimating Products

1. I have 32 students in my class. If each student has 69 colored pencils, which expression shows how many colored pencils are in my classroom?

A. 30 x 70   B. 40 x 70   C. 30 x 60

2. You have 26 Spotify playlists. If each playlist is 48 minutes long, which expression shows how many minutes of music you have?

A. 20 x 50   B. 30 x 50   C. 20 x 60

3. A veterinarian treats 19 animals every day. Which expression shows the number of animals they have treated after 31 days?

A. 40 x 10   B. 30 x 10   C. 30 x 20

4. An accountant charges a customer $89 every month. Which expression shows how much money the accountant makes after one year?

A. 90 x 10   B. 90 x 20   C. 80 x 10

5. A truck driver delivers 43 boxes to each destination they visit . If they visit 14 destinations every week, which expression shows how many boxes they deliver ?

A. 50 x 10   B. 40 x 20   C. 40 x 10

6. A cashier scans 57 items every 51 minutes. Which expression shows how many items they scan?

A. 60 x 50   B. 50 x 50   C. 60 x 60

7. You eat lunch 7 days every week. After 52 weeks, what is the expression that shows how many lunches you have eaten?

A. 10 x 60   B. 10 x 50   C. 0 x 50

8. I grade 15 tests every month. If I have 32 students, what is the expression that shows the number of tests I grade every month?

A. 10 x 30   B. 20 x 40   C. 20 x 30

9. Our school collected cans for recycling. We collected 64 bags with 88 cans inside each. What is the expression to find the total number of cans?

A. 60 x 90   B. 60 x 80   C. 70 x 90

10. A pediatrician takes care of 15 patients every day. After 66 days, what is the expression for the number of patients they have seen?

A. 10 x 70   B. 20 x 70   C. 10 x 60

***

The second common issue in promoting equity in math worksheets is missing information in word problems. This occurs when teachers forget to include information because they believe it is common knowledge.

An example is a word problem like this: Sheila is a running back on an NFL team. If she gets two touchdowns every game for the season, how many touchdowns does she have at the end? Write the equation that shows how you got your answer.

To answer this question, a student would have to know that National Football League teams play 17 games during the 18-week season. So 2 x (18-1) = 34.

People who do not know much about American football, especially at the professional level, may not know this. A rewrite of this question would include the fact that there are 18 weeks in an NFL season but Sheila's team takes one week off.

Below are before and after versions of a worksheet with similar word problems that show how to include all the relevant information for a word problem. The Common Core standard is 1.OA.2. This sheet is for addition up to 20 for first graders.

Name: _____

Addition

1. George Washington was a founding father of the US of America. If he added one amendment to the Bill of Rights, how many amendments would there be?

2. If New York City adds Long Island and Yonkers to its neighborhoods (also known as boroughs), how many boroughs will there be?

3. If the District of Columbia and Puerto Rico become states, how many stars will be on the flag?

4. A baker made a baker's dozen muffins on Monday. The baker made five more muffins on Tuesday. How many muffins did the baker make?

5. A bus pass costs $4 every day to get to work. How much will a worker spend after one week?

Name: _____

Addition

1. There are 10 amendments in the Bill of Rights. If one amendment is added to the Bill of Rights, how many amendments would there be?

2. New York City has five neighborhoods (also known as boroughs). If Long Island and Yonkers are added as new boroughs, how many boroughs will there be?

3. The US flag has 50 stars. There is one star for each state. If the District of Columbia and Puerto Rico become states, how many stars will there be on the flag?

4. A baker made a baker's dozen muffins on Monday. The baker made five more muffins on Tuesday. A baker's dozen is 13. How many muffins did the baker make?

5. A bus pass costs $4 every day to get to work. A worker goes to work five days in a seven-day week. How much will the worker spend after one week?

Science

Representation

Make sure you credit the right people for inventions. And be sure to relate noted scientists and inventions to technology or science today. Highlight the diversity in contributions in the far past, modern history, and the present.

Graphic of Historic Scientific Contributions

Asia: Paper, gunpowder, compasses, acupuncture, toothbrushes, dominoes, fireworks, silk, kites, tea

The Americans (pre-colonization): Corn, rubber, snow goggles, kayaks, hammocks, cable suspension bridges, lacrosse, baby bottles, chewing gum

Africa: Metallurgy like carbon steel, glue, jukskei (became horseshoes) Note: Because people became people in Africa and migrated outward to Asia and Europe and the Americas, many of the firsts were started in Africa, such as written languages, math and written numeric systems, medicine including pain killers and contraception, astronomy, and navigation. These things were then modernized or specialized throughout time.

Inventors

Match the invention to the inventor(s).

Lightbulb	Alexander Graham Bell and Lewis Howard Latimer
Telephone	Jawed Karim, Steven Chen, and Chad Hurley
Home security system	Lonnie G. Johnson
Automatic doors	Peter Tsai
Refrigerated trucks	Marie Van Brittan Brown
Super Soaker	Alexander Miles
USB	Shirley Jackson
YouTube	Thomas Edison and Lewis Howard Latimer
N95 respirator	Frederick McKinley Jones
Three-light traffic lights and gas masks	Garrett Morgan
Touch-tone dialing and fiber-optic cables	Ajay Bhatt

Answer Sheet

Lightbulb: Thomas Edison and Lewis Howard Latimer

Telephone: Alexander Graham Bell and Lewis Howard Latimer

Home security system: Lonnie G. Johnson

Automatic doors: Marie Van Brittan Brown

Refrigerated trucks: Frederick McKinley Jones

Super Soaker: Alexander Miles

USB: Ajay Bhatt

YouTube: Jawed Karim, Steven Chen, and Chad Hurley

N95 respirator: Peter Tsai

Three-light traffic lights and gas masks: Garrett Morgan

Touch-tone dialing and fiber-optic cables: Shirley Jackson

Experiments and Documentation

For native cultures, respect the cultural traditions and language. For example, in Hawaii, there has been a big push to return to native practices for managing fishponds. Institutions like the Nature Conservancy and the University of Hawaii are studying how native science and cultural practices have resulted in balanced ecosystems and preservation of biodiversity. Take what you know and have learned from local indigenous culture and incorporate this into your lessons. Ask questions to help students connect native science to your lesson plan. Native science is an understanding of the environment or natural world through indigenous traditions. This can be anything from how they use tally marks to a different language for animals or the approach to gardening.

Here is an activity to teach students about observation skills and the natural world around them. Take them outdoors to observe and take photos, but leave the wildlife undisturbed. You can use your phone to take photos or have students draw pictures. If you live in an urban area and do not have an outdoor space, you can have kids observe birds and insects from the window. Have students fill in what they know in a table like the one below. A related Common Core standard could be LS.1.

Name: _____

Nature Exploration

Write down the animals and plants you see.

Common Name	Native Name	Scientific Name

When you return to the classroom, you can find the other answers. You can also look up more about the animals and plants. What classification do they belong to? Are they reptiles, birds, mammals? What do they eat? How does this animal fit into the circle of life in students' own backyards or neighborhoods?

A worksheet completed by a class in Hawaii might look like this.

Nature Exploration

Write down the animals and plants you see.

Common Name	Native Name	Scientific Name
Green sea turtle	Honu	*Chelonia mydas*
Duck	Koloa	*Anas wyvilliana*
Yellow hibiscus	Pua mao hau hele	*Hibiscus brackenridgei*

Language Arts

Rubrics

As you may know, rubrics should include expectations. These make it easy for students and parents to understand what kids need to accomplish. A quantifiable rubric with clear expectations lessens the chances for subjectivity and implicit bias.

Here is an example of a narrative rubric for fifth graders. In the chart, CCSS stands for Common Core State Standards.

Narrative Rubric

	Needs Improvement (1)	Fair (2)	Good (3)	Excellent (4)
Idea and Characters (CCSS W.5.3a)	The idea and characters are not original; it is a retelling of another story.	The idea or the characters are original.	The idea and most of the characters are original.	The idea and characters are both original.
Sentence Fluency (CCSS W.5.3c)	Most sentences are incomplete or short.	Sentences are short and do not have sentence openers.	Sentences vary in length with repetitive sentence openers.	Sentences vary in length and structure. Writing is natural and smooth. Different sentence openers are used.
Organization (CCSS W.5.3, W.5.3e)	There is no identifiable beginning, middle, or end.	One is identifiable: beginning, middle, or end.	Two are identifiable: beginning, middle, or end.	All three are identifiable: beginning, middle, and end.
Use of Five Senses (CCSS W.5.3d)	Student uses two or fewer senses in the details.	Student uses three senses in the details.	Student uses four senses in the details.	Student uses all five senses in the details.

Narrative Rubric

	Needs Improvement (1)	Fair (2)	Good (3)	Excellent (4)
Spacing and Font	Student does not use the proper spacing, font, or font size between words and sentences.	Student sometimes uses the proper spacing, font, and/or font size between words and sentences.	Student mostly uses the proper spacing, font, and font size between words and sentences.	Student always uses the proper spacing, font, and/or font size between words and sentences.

You'll notice that information on expectations in terms of spelling, grammar, punctuation, and capitalization is missing. I do encourage you to highlight these issues in the actual paper and offer corrections. However, students may be using AAVE/BVE or Spanish/Spanglish, or are not native English speakers. If you can understand the meaning of the word in the context of the sentence, then err on the side of guidance.

If students here are making similar, frequent mistakes in spelling or punctuation, make a handout for students that illustrates the American English versions. Give students the opportunity to correct grammar, punctuation, and spelling that you have pointed out and turn in their stories again.

Fun Fact

Even punctuation varies from language to language. Some European countries use a period instead of a comma when writing numbers. So 1,000 becomes 1.000. The Greek question mark looks like a semicolon. Then there are cultural differences. For ellipses, many young people are also using ,,, instead of the usual ...

Social Studies

Geography and Maps

When you teach geography, check out maps from less Euro-centric perspectives. Share what the world looks like in globe form as well. Did you know that Africa and Antarctica are actually larger than usually shown? Check out the map online at https://thetruesize.com for a visual.

When teaching geography and capitals, make sure to include other countries besides European ones.

History

Discovery versus Exploration

When talking about history and the Age of Exploration, make sure to use the term "exploration" instead of "discovery" because European explorers never really discovered inhabited places. Because these are younger children, it is not necessary to go into detail about the servitude or occupation that came with colonization. However, kids will understand how disease spread and how they did not have masks or the kinds of vaccines we have. You can talk about how disease spread through native populations because the people did not have immunity.

Prehistoric and Indigenous First

When you teach history, start with the history before the Age of Exploration. For the mainland of the US and Alaska, talk about how one theory is that Indigenous Americans crossed the land bridge from Eurasia and spread downward. It should be noted that there are theories that people of the Americas had contact with sea voyagers from Africa or Asia even before that. For Hawaii and American Samoa, the theory is the people came from the islands in Asia, like the Philippines, and sailed from island to island through Micronesia to the Pacific. Learn about the local tribe in your specific area and what that tribe did before Europeans arrived.

Time Line

25,000 years ago: People crossed the land bridge to North America

1492: Christopher Columbus lands in the Bahamas

1513: Ponce de Leon lands in Florida

1526–1865: Slavery in American territories

1760–1840: Industrial Revolution

1763: First recorded settlement of Asians in North America is Filipinos in Louisiana

1765–1791: American Revolution

1790: Naturalization Act says only Whites can be citizens

1791: Haiti Revolution

1805: Meriwether Lewis, William Clark, and Sacagawea start their journey

1807: The Act Prohibiting Importation of Slaves

1812: War of 1812

1827–1838: Muscogee Nation removal

1830: Indian Removal Act

1831: Nat Turner rebellion

1838: Potawatomi Trail of Death

1838–1850: Trail of Tears

1846–1848: Mexican-American War

1848–1855: California gold rush

1851: Indian Appropriations Act

1854: California Supreme Court rules that Chinese cannot testify against Whites

1860: Last slave ship

1861–1865: Civil War

1863: Emancipation Proclamation

1863–1866: Long Walk of the Navajo

1865: States begin leasing prisoners to businessmen

1865–1954: Segregation

1867: Alaska is sold to US by Russia

1870: Naturalization Act says only Whites and Blacks can be citizens

1882: Chinese Exclusion Act

1890: Wounded Knee Massacre

1893: Overthrow of Kingdom of Hawaii

1898: Hawaii is annexed by US

1898: US military takes Puerto Rico during Spanish-American War

1914–1918: World War I

1917: Puerto Ricans became American citizens

1920: Women are allowed to vote

1921: Tulsa race massacre

1924: Indian Citizenship Act

1929–1939: Great Depression

1932: Tuskegee Experiment

1934: Indian Reorganization Act

1939–1945: World War II

1941: Pearl Harbor bombing

1941–1945: The Holocaust

1942: Removal of Aleut villagers

1942–1945: Japanese American internment camps

1947–1989: Cold War

1950–1953: Korean War

1954: *Brown v. Board of Education*

1955–1975: Vietnam War

1957: Little Rock Nine

1959: Hawaii and Alaska become states

1960s: Civil Rights Movement

1961: Freedom Rides

1963: March on Washington

1964: Civil Rights Act

1965: Voting Rights Act

1968: Indian Civil Rights Act

1968: Fair Housing Act

1970s: Information Age starts

1975: Indian Self-Determination and Education Act

1978: Indian Child Welfare Act

1978: American Indian Religious Freedom Act

1988: Civil Liberties Act, which gives a formal apology and $20,000 in compensation to Asian Americans who had been interned in camps

1988: Indian Gaming Regulatory Act

1989: World Wide Web is invented

1990: Native American Graves Protection and Repatriation Act

1993: US apologizes for overthrow of Kingdom of Hawaii

1997: Apology for Tuskegee Experiment

2001: 9/11 attacks

2001–2021: War in Afghanistan

2007–2009: Great Recession

2008: President Barack Obama is elected

2008: US House of Representatives apologizes for slavery and Jim Crow laws

2010: US apologizes to Indigenous Americans

2011: Defense of Marriage Act is deemed unconstitutional

2013: Trayvon Martin is killed

2014: Black Lives Matter is founded after Michael Brown and Eric Garner are killed by police

2015: Same-sex marriage is legal nationwide

2017–2021: Trump travel ban

2020: COVID-19 hits and in US kills people of color disproportionately

2021: Vice President Kamala Harris takes office

Timeline Tournament

To help your students gain a better perspective on history, especially for the visual learners, use the Timeline Classic card game by Zygomatic (or create your own) with your class. Basically, you have cards that have an event or an invention on one side. On the other side is the date the event or invention happened. Players are dealt a hand and take turns putting down their cards, guessing the order, and seeing if they are correct. The first one to guess all their cards correctly wins.

Do a bracket tournament in your classroom. While some students are competing, review old cards with other students to learn about the event/invention and how it relates to people today.

Expand the Important People

Teach about more than the usual suspects when it comes to people of color. I mean, obviously, cover Martin Luther King Jr. and Rosa Parks, but do not limit the achievements of people of color. This goes especially for when the events you are covering are events in which a White man ends up as the hero, like signing an emancipation. Otherwise, you risk playing into the idea of a White savior.

When you teach about slavery, teach about the people who led rebellions alongside Harriet Tubman and the Underground Railroad. Check out Nat Turner, Gabriel Prosser, and Denmark Vesey.

When you teach about the Civil Rights Movement, include Malcolm X, Baynard Rustin, César Chávez, and Yuri Kochiyama.

This worksheet gives offers a brief an overview of the different attitudes of the Civil Rights Movement in the 1960s and shows how so many groups were working for equality in their own ways. Over time, their opinions changed on how equality should be reached and what equality looked like. The Civil Rights Movement was also larger than equality between Blacks and Whites, and/or segregation. There were anti-war sentiments, women's rights, gay rights, Latino rights, and union and labor parties. Even today, the fight continues for civil rights on the same subjects—socialism, prison system reform, education reform, Puerto Rico's representation, and police brutality.

The people that fought for these rights came from all different backgrounds and races. They overlapped in their beliefs and support for one another.

Name: _____

Who Am I?

Match the name to the Civil Rights Movement leader.

Martin Luther King, Jr.   Baynard Rustin

Yuri Kochiyama   Malcolm X

Angela Davis   César Chávez

	• Was a Christian minister • Gave the "I Have a Dream" speech • Stood for nonviolence • Wanted to get rid of segregation
	• Grew up in foster care • Leader in the Nation of Islam • Believed Black people should protect themselves • Opposed integration
	• Founded the National Farm Workers Association • Believed in nonviolence • Wanted to raise pay and improve working conditions for farm workers • Led the Delano grape strike
	• Believed in nonviolence • Co-organized the Southern Christian Leadership Conference • Organized the March on Washington • Advocated for gay rights

Who Am I?

	• Experienced life in a US internment camp • Was an activist for Black nationalism and anti-war efforts • Believed in Puerto Rican independence • Fought against racial profiling of South Asians after 9/11
	• Studied French and philosophy • Was a feminist and member of the Black Panther Party • Became a professor at the University of California • Criticized the prison system

This worksheet offers a brief look into the different attitudes of the Civil Rights Movement in the 1960s and shows how so many groups were working for equality in their own ways. Over time, their opinions changed on how equality should be reached and what equality looked like. The Civil Rights Movement was also larger than equality between Blacks and Whites, and/or segregation. There were anti-war sentiments, women's rights, gay rights, Latino rights, and union and labor parties. Even today, the fight continues for civil rights on the same subjects, such as socialism, prison system reform, education reform, Puerto Rico's representation, and police brutality.

The people that fought for these rights came from all different backgrounds and races. They overlapped in their beliefs and support for one another.

Chapter 9

MINI LESSON PLANS

Kindergarten

Subject: Seasons and Social Studies

Lesson Title: What Do We Wear in the Cold?

Skills/Common Core Standards: CCSS.ELA-Literacy. SL.K.3, CCSS.ELA-Literacy.SL.K.4, CCSS.ELA-Literacy. SL.K.6

Objectives	Resources/Materials
• Understand cold weather and proper attire in your hometown • Discuss cold weather and proper attire in other parts of the US • Examine the differences and similarities between cultures	• Your own cold weather clothes • Photos of winter clothes across the US • Annual winter forecast on the Accuweather website • Paper and crayons

Activity

Introduction: Ask students what happens in the winter. What is the weather like? Ask students what they wear when it is cold outside. As students give answers, show your cold weather clothing items, like gloves, a hat, a scarf, and more.

Instruction/Interaction: Ask students what they think people wear in the winter in Florida, in Alaska, in Hawaii. Listen to their ideas for each place. Talk about how cold or not cold some places can get. Use Accuweather's current winter forecast online to show students what winter can feel like in other places. Icy? Dry? Warm? Snowy?

Point out places that are different from your hometown. Use modern-day photos of Indigenous and local people to show what they wear in the winter in their areas.

Point out places in the US not shown on the map.

Alaska—Inuit people, especially women, wear the amauti parka, which lets them stay warm and carry their kids on their back to keep them warm. In general, people in Alaska wear heavier boots, gloves, and coats because of how cold it can get.

Hawaii—Most people still wear sandals (called slippers there), swimsuits, shorts, and other summer clothes when down on the lower elevation. If they go up a mountain, they wear winter clothes because it can snow up there. Some people even snowboard. Some people put snow in their pickup trucks and drive it down to the beach to make snowmen.

Activity: If you could try a different kind of winter, what would that be? Draw yourself in that place.

Reflection

1. How is the weather different in other places? How is it similar?

2. How does the weather change what people wear?

3. What is your favorite piece of winter clothing?

Grade One

Subject: Counting and Money

Lesson Title: Beads around the World

Skills/Common Core Standards: CCSS.ELA-Literacy.L.1.6, CCSS.ELA-Literacy.SL.1.1.b, CCSS.Math.Content.1.NBT.C.4

Objectives	Resources/Materials
• Explore past and present methods of payment • Understand how trade has affected communities and how it still affects us today	• An old debit card • Cash and coins • Beads and string • Photos of beadwork on display at museums • Photos of current-day beadwork

Activity

Introduction: Ask students to talk about how their parents pay for items when at the checkout at a store. Tell them to discuss this in small groups for five minutes. After five minutes, ask volunteers for answers. As students give answers, show your physical example of the item they say. If you feel comfortable, pass it around the class.

Instruction: Ask students what people did before there was money. Today, we can use our phones with Apple Pay or Google Pay or we can use cards. Some people still use cash. Even fewer people use checks. Explain the concept of trading goods and services. Explain how beads were one of the things traded in the Americas, Africa, China, and Indonesia before paper money or coins. Instead of plastic, beads were made out of glass or ceramics, and beads were not always available. This is one reason why beading became so important in traditional artwork and clothing. Show pictures of the different kinds of beads from across the globe and how they were used.

Ask students where they see beads today. Some students may say bracelets, necklaces, and earrings. Black students may say waist beads. American Indian students may speak about certain colors or patterns to represent tribes. Chinese American students may know about jade beads that are passed down. In Polynesian cultures, they use shells as beads. Someone's grandparents may embroider with beads. Show students examples of today's beadwork.

Activity: Give students an assortment of beads and string. Let them barter or trade for the color or kind they want. Then instruct them to make a pattern into a necklace, a bracelet, or another accessory.

Reflection

1. What feelings did you have when you traded beads?

2. Were there some beads that everyone wanted more than others?

3. How did these feelings or the beads you had change your pattern?

4. What does your pattern mean to you?

Grade Two

Subject: Reading and Social Studies

Lesson Title: Neighborhoods–Same or Different?

Skills/Common Core Standards: CC.2.R.L.1, CC.2.R.L.6

Objectives	Resources/Materials
• Compare and contrast neighborhoods • Learn to use context clues to predict a story	• *My Papi Has a Motorcycle* by Isabel Quintero • Pictures of your neighborhood

Activity

Introduction: Show students photos of your neighborhood and, if you have them, your neighbors. What stores are there? What people do you see? Are there many roads and cars? Or are there farms? Or something in between?

Ask students about their community. Where do they like to eat? What do they see when they go to school? Tell them to keep this in mind as you read.

Introduce the book and preview it. What might the story be about? Who might be the main character be?

Reading: As you read, check in on what the girl smells, sees, and hears around her neighborhood. Do your students see, smell, or hear similar things in their neighborhoods? What might happen next? What language are they speaking? Do you need to look up a word like panaderia?

Reflection

1. Where did this story take place? Could this story take place in your neighborhood? In your city or state?

2. What was the story about?

3. Who were the main characters?

4. How is their neighborhood the same or different from yours?

Grade Three

Subject: Language Arts

Lesson Title: What Is a Poem?

Skills/Common Core Standards: CC.3.R.L.5

Objectives	Resources/Materials
• Analyze the meaning of a poem • Learn three different types of poems	• A Dr. Seuss book • A nursery rhyme • *Brown Girl Dreaming* by Jacqueline Woodson • A recent, popular (kid-friendly) song • "Over the Wintry" by Natsume Sōseki • "There Was an Old Man with a Beard" by Edward Lear

Activity

Introduction: Establish what your students know about poems already. What counts as a poem? What kinds of poems are there?

Instruction: Go over the types of poems that they may have seen before, such as a nursery rhyme or a Dr. Seuss book. Point out that songs can be poems. Show also how poems don't always have to rhyme and sometimes tell long stories with *Brown Girl Dreaming*. Introduce two simple poems created in different countries: Japanese haikus and Irish limericks.

Go over what makes a haiku (5-7-5 syllables in three lines) or a limerick (AABBA rhyme scheme in five lines). Analyze the two poems "Over the Wintry" and "There Was an Old Man with a Beard." What could they mean?

Activity: Have students write their own haiku or limerick or one stanza of a song.

Reflection

When students are done with their poems, have a few students share. Work as a class to analyze the possible meaning of the poem before asking the student what they meant. Show how analysis can be right and wrong at the same time, depending on who is reading.

Grade Four

Subject: Social Studies and History

Lesson Title: Who Was Here First?

Skills/Common Core Standards: CC.4.R.I.10

Objectives	Resources/Materials
• Determine what tribes settled your home state first • Identify what life was like before European settlers	• List of federal-and-state-recognized tribes on the National Conference of State Legislators website • Local tribal website with photos or paintings of cultural items and traditions • Computer/internet • Notepad and paper

Activity

Introduction: Ask students how long their family has lived in this state. Ask students who were the first people who lived in their state.

Instruction: Name the tribe or tribes who lived in the area. Usually, a tribe website will give a history of the food they ate, their traditions, their clothes, and their homes.

Activity: Have students research the local American Indian tribe online and take notes. Note that this can be made into a longer-form project like a diorama or a short essay.

Reflection

1. What did you learn about the people who lived here first?
2. What is something we have in common? What is different?
3. What is this tribe or tribes doing now?

Grade Five

Subject: Social Studies and History

Lesson Title: Slavery as Told by Former Slaves

Skills/Common Core Standards: CC.5.SL.1.d

Objectives	Resources/Materials
Understand US history with slavery from a slave perspective	*Born in Slavery: Slave Narratives from the Federal Writers' Project, 1936 to 1938*

Activity

Introduction: Review what a primary source is. Introduce the *Slave Narratives* book. Former slaves were interviewed by journalists and asked a series of questions between 1936 and 1938. Many of the former slaves were elderly, but they did recall what it was like. Several states took part in this project, so you can possibly read stories from your own state. This material is public domain, so it is available online for free.

Instruction: As you read, stop to ask what question you think the interviewer asked. Ask your students to reflect on why the interviewer may be asking these questions. Read three short narratives. In the Ohio collection, I would choose Susan Bledsoe, Fleming Clark, and Ben Brown. These accounts do not have the N-word in them or graphic violence. The plantations and slave treatments are varied as well.

Activity: Have a group discussion about the lives of the ex-slaves. What did they remember? What did they have in common? What was different? How do you think their lives changed after they were free? Why do you think most slaves, no matter how they were treated, said they were happy to be free?

Reflection

This group discussion can lead to future lessons on these topics:

- Issues of civil rights that last until today
- The Juneteenth holiday and how ex-slaves celebrated
- The Thirteenth Amendment
- The Reconstruction era

You can also use the group discussion as a jumping-off point to work backwards to cover these topics:

- Atlantic triangular trade and how slaves came to the US
- How slaves fought for freedom/the abolitionist movement before and during the war
- The Civil War and the Emancipation Proclamation

Chapter 10

LISTS OF MATERIALS

Books

Not all of the books below are written by authors of the listed race category. I chose to still include these books because the content and quality of the story is well done, and the stories are widely accessible in public libraries. Literature that is written with a central character of color by writers of color of this kind is still sparse—not from a lack of writers, but from a lack of supportive publishers. Note that these lists are not exhaustive.

If you cannot find these books in the library and do not have the ability to purchase them, they can also be found on YouTube. Librarians and other educators read these books aloud there.

Picture Books for Lower Elementary

You'll see in this list that many of these books are not about festivals or historic events. It is important to have characters of every race doing everyday American or childhood things. The characters in these books may see the world and interpret it through the lens of someone of their race or culture, but the main focus is not a performative aspect of their culture. It is daily life.

Black

- *The Proudest Blue: A Story of Hijab and Family* by Ibtihaj Muhammad
- *Ruby Finds a Worry* by Tom Percival
- *Not Quite Snow White* by Ashley Franklin
- *Parker Looks Up: An Extraordinary Moment* by Parker Curry and Jessica Curry
- *Grace for President* by Kelly DiPucchio
- *Thank You, Omu* by Oge Mora
- *Max and the Tag-Along Moon* by Floyd Cooper
- *Love Is* by Diane Adams
- *Just Like Me* by Vanessa Brantley-Newton

Asian

- *Grandmother's Visit* by Betty Quan
- *Hush! A Thai Lullaby* by Minfong Ho
- *A Different Pond* by Bao Phi
- *Eyes That Kiss in the Corners* by Joanna Ho
- *Emma's Rug* by Allen Say
- *My Footprints* by Bao Phi
- *Big Red Lollipop* by Rukhsana Khan
- *Hana Hashimoto, Sixth Violin* by Chieri Uegaki
- *Mama's Saris* by Pooja Makhijani

Latino

- *Islandborn* by Junot Díaz
- *Areli Is a Dreamer: A True Story* by Areli Morales
- *Across the Bay* by Carlos Aponte
- *Carmela Full of Wishes* by Matt de la Peña
- *Nosotros Means Us: A Bilingual Story* by Paloma Valdivia
- *Just Ask! Be Different, Be Brave, Be You* by Sonia Sotomayor
- *Alma and How She Got Her Name* by Juana Martinez-Neal
- *Listening with My Heart: A Story of Kindness and Self-Compassion* by Gabi Garcia
- *Evelyn Del Rey Is Moving Away* by Meg Medina
- *My Papi Has a Motorcycle* by Isabel Quintero
- *Dancing Hands: How Teresa Carreño Played the Piano for President Lincoln* by Margarita Engle
- *La Princesa and the Pea* by Susan Middleton Elya
- *Coquí in the City* by Nomar Perez

Indigenous American

- *Zoe and the Fawn* by Catherine Jameson
- *When We Are Kind* by Monique Gray Smith
- *We Are Water Protectors* by Carole Lindstrom
- *SkySisters* by Jan Bourdeau Waboose
- *Wild Berries* by Julie Flett
- *I Sang You Down from the Stars* by Tasha Spillett-Sumner
- *Yetsa's Sweater* by Sylvia Olsen
- *At the Mountain's Base* by Traci Sorell

- *Thunder Boy Jr.* by Sherman Alexie
- *Stolen Words* by Melanie Florence
- *Mama, Do you Love Me?* by Barbara M. Joosse,
- *Ohana Means Family* by Ilima Loomis
- *Too Many Mangos* by Tammy Paikai
- *Keala and the Hawaiian Bird* by Patricia McLean

Bilingual/Immigrant

- *Cool Salsa: Bilingual Poems on Growing Up Latino in the US,* edited by Lori M. Carlson
- *Where Are You From?* by Yamile Saied Méndez
- *The Name Jar* by Yangsook Choi
- *Mama's Nightingale: A Story of Immigration and Separation* by Edwidge Danticat
- *One Green Apple* by Eve Bunting
- *Dreamers* by Yuyi Morales
- *My Diary from Here to There* by Amada Irma Pérez
- *My Shoes and I* by René Colato Laíinez
- *Hannah Is My Name: A Young Immigrant's Story* by Belle Yang

Older children also benefit from books that are not solely focused on their race, but incorporative. Their differences are important but not their whole story or identity.

Books for Upper Elementary

Black

- *Listen, Layla* by Yassmin Abdel-Magied
- *As Brave as You* by Jason Reynolds

- *Brown Girl Dreaming* by Jacqueline Woodson
- *One Crazy Summer* by Rita Williams-Garcia
- *Kickoff!* by Tiki Barber, Ronde Barber, and Paul Mantell
- *Two Naomis* by Olugbemisola Rhuday-Perkovich and Audrey Vernick
- *New Kid* by Jerry Craft

Asian

- *Always Anjali* by Sheetal Sheth
- *A Map into the World* by Kao Kalia Yang
- *Stand Up, Yumi Chung!* by Jessica Kim
- *Front Desk by* Kelly Yang
- *Step Up to the Plate, Maria Singh* by Uma Krishnaswami
- *Tall Story* by Candy Gourlay

Latino

- *The Way to Rio Luna* by Zoraida Córdova
- *Ghost Squad* by Claribel A. Ortega
- *Lety Out Loud: A Wish Novel* by Angela Cervantes
- *Gaby, Lost and Found* by Angela Cervantes
- *How Tía Lola Came to Stay* by Julia Alvarez

Indigenous American

- *I Can Make This Promise* by Christine Day
- *Red Bird Sings: The Story of Zitkala-Ša, Native American Author, Musician, and Activist* by Gina Capaldi and Q. L. Pearce
- *The Warriors* by Joseph Bruchac

- *The Reluctant Storyteller* by Art Coulson
- *The Shark King* by R. Kikuo Johnson

Bilingual/Immigrant

- *A Kids Book About Immigration* by M. J. Calderon
- *Inside Out and Back Again* by Thanhhaā Lai
- *Pie in the Sky* by Remy Lai
- *The Only Road* by Alexandra Diaz
- *Other Words for Home* by Jasmine Warga
- *When Stars Are Scattered* by Victoria Jamieson and Omar Mohamed
- *Shooting Kabul* by N. H. Senzai
- *Sea Prayer* by Khaled Hosseini
- *Return to Sender* by Julia Alvarez

Historical Events Books Reading List for Upper Elementary Students

This reading list focuses on commonly misrepresented or underrepresented holidays and events in history. Some of these books can be read to lower elementary students, but they should have guidance and explanation from the teacher. Some of the books are nonfiction, and others are historical fiction.

You'll notice that the usual suspects (Martin Luther King Jr., Rosa Parks, Pocahontas, Sacagawea) are not included. These famous icons probably have enough coverage in your classroom.

Thanksgiving

- *The Very First Americans* by Cara Ashrose
- *We Are Grateful* by Traci Sorell
- *The Circle of Thanks* by Joseph Bruchac
- *Squanto's Journey: The Story of the First Thanksgiving* by Joseph Bruchac
- *1621: A New Look at Thanksgiving* by Catherine O'Neill Grace and Margaret M. Bruchac

Trail of Tears/Genocide

- *Mary and the Trail of Tears: A Cherokee Removal Survival Story* by Andrea L. Rogers
- *How I Became a Ghost: A Choctaw Trail of Tears Story* by Tim Tingle
- *Soft Rain: A Story of the Cherokee Trail of Tears* by Cornelia Cornelissen
- *The Birchbark House* by Louise Erdrich
- *Malian's Song* by Marge Bruchac

Boarding Schools and Indigenous Erasure

- *I Am Not a Number* by Jenny Kay Dupuis and Kathy Kacer
- *When We Were Alone* by David A. Robertson
- *Shi-shi-etko* by Nicola I. Campbell
- *Shin-chi's Canoe* by Nicola I. Campbell

Slavery

- *Before She Was Harriet* by Lesa Cline-Ransome
- *Henry's Freedom Box: A True Story from the Underground Railroad* by Ellen Levine
- *Show Way* by Jacqueline Woodson
- *The Patchwork Path: A Quilt Map to Freedom* by Bettye Stroud
- *The Poet Slave of Cuba: A Biography of Juan Francisco Manzano* by Margarita Engle

Civil Rights

- *Ron's Big Mission* by Rose Blue and Corinne J. Naden
- *Ruth and the Green Book* by Calvin Alexander Ramsey and Gwen Strauss
- *Child of the Civil Rights Movement* by Paula Young Shelton
- *The Other Side* by Jacqueline Woodson
- *Separate Is Never Equal: Sylvia Mendez and Her Family's Fight for Desegregation* by Duncan Tonatiuh
- *Sylvia and Aki* by Winifred Conkling

Gold Rush/Immigration

- *Coolies* by Yin
- *Kai's Journey to Gold Mountain: An Angel Island Story* by Katrina Saltonstall Currier
- *The Gold Rush: Chinese Immigrants Come to America (1848–1882)* by Jeremy Thornton
- *Grandfather's Journey* by Allen Say
- *Wishes* by Mượn Thị Văn

Japanese Internment

- *A Place Where Sunflowers Grow* by Amy Lee-Tai
- *Fish for Jimmy: Inspired by One Family's Experience in a Japanese American Internment Camp* by Katie Yamasaki
- *Fred Korematsu Speaks Up* by Laura Atkins and Stan Yogi
- *Passage to Freedom: The Sugihara Story* by Ken Mochizuki
- *The Bracelet* by Yoshiko Uchida

Kingdom of Hawaii and Hawaii in World War II

- *Kaiulani: The People's Princess, Hawaii, 1889* by Ellen Emerson White
- *Lydia and the Island Kingdom: A Story Based on the Real Life of Princess Liliuokalani of Hawaii* by Joan Holub
- *Prints in the Sand: My Journey with Nanea* by Erin Falligant

Puerto Rico

- *In the Shade of the Nispero Tree* by Carmen T. Bernier-Grand
- *Schomburg: The Man Who Built a Library* by Carole Boston Weatherford
- *Parrots over Puerto Rico* by Susan L. Roth and Cindy Trumbore
- *The Storyteller's Candle* by Lucía M. González and Lulu Delacre
- *Planting Stories: The Life of Librarian and Storyteller Pura Belpré* by Anika Aldamuy Denise

Kids Books for Historical Figures of Color

- Who Was/Who Is series—You have to do some digging, but the books do cover the more uncommon people of color, like Che Guevara, Maria Tallchief, Nelson Mandela, Roberto Clemente, Sitting Bull, Booker T. Washington, and more.

- Little Leaders and Leaders and Dreamers series—There are several books on accomplished Black women, accomplished Black men, and accomplished women of color.

- Little People, Big Dreams series—You can search for BIPOC on the Little People, Big Dreams website, and there are a few books about lesser-known people, such as Wilma Rudolph, Jean-Michel Basquiat, Zaha Hadid, Pelé, and Evonne Goolagong.

- She Persisted series—This series even includes Spanish translations and features women like Marian Anderson, Patsy Mink, Wangari Maathai, Claudette Colvin, Florence Griffith Joyner, and more.

- *Black Women in Science* by Kimberly Brown Pellum

- *Asian-Americans Who Inspire Us* by Analiza Quiroz Wolf

- *Awesome Asian Americans: 20 Stars Who Made America Amazing* by Phil Amara and Oliver Chin

- *Stories for South Asian Supergirls* by Raj Kaur Khaira

- *Nuestra América: 30 Inspiring Latinas/Latinos Who Have Shaped the US* by Sabrina Vourvoulias

- *Courageous History Makers: 11 Women from Latin America Who Changed the World* by Naibe Reynoso

- *Fearless Trailblazers: 11 Latinos Who Made US History* by Naibe Reynoso

Online Resources

Smithsonian Teaching Resources

- Smithsonian Asian Pacific American Center
  https://smithsonianapa.org/learn

- Smithsonian Latino Center
  https://learninglab.si.edu/profile/latinocenter

- National Museum of the American Indian
  https://learninglab.si.edu/org/nmaahc

- National Museum of African American History and Culture
  https://nmaahc.si.edu

TikTok

Black

- #blackhistoryfacts
- @_lyneezy Lynae Vanee
- @kahlilgreene Kahlil Greene
- @ndcpoetry Nick Courmon

Asian

- #asianamerican
- #asianamericanlife
- #StopAsianHate
- @janeparkang Jane Park
- @aolinekyne Kyne
- @imtiffanyyu Tiffany Yu

Latino

- #latinostiktok
- @AfroLatinxUnited
- @ciscoviera Cisco
- @fernandacortesx Fernanda Cortes

Indigenous American

- #indigenoustiktok
- #nativetiktok
- #hawaiian
- @shinanova Shina Novalinga
- @notoriouscree James Jones
- @tiamiscihk Tia Wood
- @kuakamahao Kamahaʻo

Digital Classroom Connections

The best way to connect with another classroom in a different country is to create a sister-school relationship. Many times this requires working with administration. It's not impossible to do it yourself from one teacher to another, especially if you know a teacher or alum who is teaching overseas. After creating a relationship with an overseas teacher, utilize one of the many video conferencing platforms to connect your classrooms digitally.

Another option to connect is through PenPal Schools, a website with educational topics, videos, and prompt questions. In a chat after each video, you can see what other students from around the world have written.

Remember to check time zones if you want to do a live chat. If you're in the eastern standard time zone, you share a time zone with students in Cuba, Haiti, Venezuela, Bolivia, and parts of Brazil. Much of Central America and Mexico share central standard time. Some of Western Mexico and Northwestern Canada share mountain standard time. While they are not on the same time zone, Hawaii, much of Alaska, and the Aluetian Islands are on similar time zones with only one hour difference

Topics are for third-grade students and up. These topic titles include Schools around the World, World Explorer, Oceans, World News, Protecting the Planet, and many more. The drawback is that there is very little regulation of who signs up as a teacher.

Equity Support Systems for Teachers

Lean In: Join a Lean In circle. Lean In is a website for women working for equality. The circles connect women in similar circumstances and provide information for anti-racism tactics and support like mentorship.
leanin.org

Teaching for Equity: Teaching for Equity through Leading Educators is a professional-development program and guide with coaching and sessions for school systems and educators.
https://leadingeducators.org/equity

Educators for Equity/Envision Equality: For financial support, you can apply for an Educators for Equity grant through the nonprofit NWEA (Northwest Evaluation Association). This is open to schools across the US.

The NEA Foundation has an Envision Equity grant with spring, summer, and winter applications.
https://www.nwea.org/our-mission/educators-for-equity

Other Online Resources

We Need Diverse Books: The Resources page of this organization's website includes links for lists of diverse books by ethnicity and religion, a link to diverse book subscription boxes, and a page of diverse-owned bookstores in the US listed by state.
https://diversebooks.org

The History You Didn't Learn series by *Time*: This video series includes such topics as Black Wall Street, the health programs started by the Black Panthers, Latinas in the labor movement, and Angel Island, which was like California's Ellis Island and served as a processing station for Chinese and other immigrants

Kids Meet: YouTube channel HiHo Kids is home to the Kids Meet series, in which children of varied ages meet different kinds of people, including a former Black Panther, a survivor of a Japanese American internment camp, a refugee, a Holocaust survivor, and more.

Op-Docs from the *New York Times*: This video series features conversations with people on the subject of race; you can search for "a conversation with" for every race.
www.nytimes.com/video/op-docs

"27 Mistakes White Teachers of Black Students Make and How to Fix Them": This blog post by Jay Wamsted on the Education Post website is full of helpful links.
https://educationpost.org/27-mistakes-White-teachers-of-black-students-make-and-how-to-fix-them

Learning for Justice: This organization's website has a section for Teaching Hard History that includes topics like slavery for kindergarten through grade five. It has videos, podcasts, frameworks, and more resources for teachers. https://www.learningforjustice.org/frameworks/teaching-hard-history/american-slavery

Examples of Notable BIPOC

	Politics	Activism	Science
Black	Kamala Harris	Alicia Garza	Dorothy Johnson Vaughan
Latino	Alexandria Ocasio-Cortez	Emma González	Ellen Ochoa
East Asian	David Ige	Yuji Ichioka	Flossie Wong-Staal
Indigenous American	Debra Anne Haaland	Cierra Fields	Aaron Yazzie
South Asian	Rashida Tlaib	Malala Yousafzai	Kalpana Chawla
Southeast Asian	Bobby Scott	Philip Vera Cruz	Rampa Rattanarithikul

	Art*	Business
Black	Jean-Michel Basquiat	Sevetri Wilson
Latino	Lin-Manuel Miranda	Jordi Munoz
East Asian	Amy Tan	Eric Yuan
Indigenous American	Aku-Matu	Madonna Yawakie
South Asian	Jhumpa Lahiri	Niraj Shah
Southeast Asian	Viet Thanh Nguyen	Sheila Lirio Marcelo

* Note that the list of artists does not include the arts that minorities are stereotypically associated with, like rap, music, and acting. Children can recognize early on that Hollywood fame may be difficult to attain.

Popular Female Names of Color to Replace White Female Names*

Alphabet	Black	Latina	Indigenous American	Asian
A	Aliyah	Ariana	Amka	Aki
B	Breonna	Belinda	—	Bo
C	Chanise	Camila	Chepi	Chiaki
D	Deja	Delfina	Dakota	Diu
E	Ebony	Elisa	Elu	Esha
F	Fajah	Francesca	Fala	Fatimah
G	Gabrielle	Guadalupe	—	Guan-Yin
H	Henrietta	Hermelinda	Hialeah	Hitomi
I	Imani	Isabella	Isi	Ishani
J	Jada	Julieta	—	Jia
K	Kiara	Karla	Kallik	Kamala
L	Laila	Luciana	Leilani	Ladli
M	Monifa	Martina	Malie	Mei
N	Nia	Natalia	Nanouk	Nira
O	Octavia	Ofelia	Odina	—
P	Precious	Paula	Pualani	Prisha
Q	Queen	—	—	Quy
R	Raven	Rafaela	—	Rudee
S	Shanice	Sofia	Shako	Sahana
T	Tia	Tatiana	Tapeesa	Tien
U	Ulena	—	Uki	Urja
V	Valeria	Victoria	—	Varsha
W	Wanda	—	Walela	Wattana
X	—	Ximena	—	Xiao Chen
Y	Yevette	Yesenia	—	Yumi
Z	Zekia	Zara	Zaltana	Zahira

* Some spaces are blank because that letter is not popular for certain races or genders.

Popular Male Names of Color to Replace White Male Names*

Alphabet	Black	Latino	Indigenous American	Asian
A	Andre	Angel	Adohi	Ang
B	Booker	Bruno	Bidziil	Bao
C	Cassius	Cortez	Chayton	Chen
D	Darius	Diego	Dustu	Decha
E	Elijah	Emiliano	Enoli	Emmad
F	Freddie	Felipe	—	Feng
G	Garfield	Gael	Gaagii	Giang
H	Hakeen	Hugo	Hiawatha	Hasan
I	Isaiah	Ignacio	Inuksuk	Isamu
J	Jamal	Julian	Jacy	Jin
K	Keith	—	Kaimana	Kumail
L	Lamonte	Liam	Lokela	Lim
M	Marquis	Mateo	Makani	Makoto
N	Naeem	Navarro	Nahele	Nikhil
O	Omari	Oliverio	Ori	Osamu
P	Philandro	Pablo	Pika	Piyush
Q	Quinton	—	—	Qiu
R	Rashon	Rodrigo	Rowtag	Ren
S	Stephon	Sebastián	Shappa	Sanjay
T	Trayvon	Thiago	Tyee	Takashi
U	Umar	—	Uzumati	Uday
V	Vashan	Vicente	Viho	Vidura
W	Willie	—	Wohali	Wu
X	Xavier	Ximeno	—	Xuan
Y	—	Yandel	Yona	Yuan
Z	Zion	Zacarias	—	Zinan

* Some spaces are blank because that letter is not popular for certain races or genders.

Information on How to Talk about Race in the Classroom

These resources are for teachers, not for elementary students.

- "PBS Kids Talk About Race, Racism, and Identity"
  https://www.youtube.com/watch?v=B5moq6_5LSk

- "How to Talk to Kids About Race"
  https://www.youtube.com/watch?v=QNEKbVq_ou4

- "How Four Educators Prepare for Conversations About Race and Racism in the Classroom"
  https://www.youtube.com/watch?v=PJ19pxC_bVg

- "Black Student Voices: Classroom Discussions on Race"
  https://www.youtube.com/watch?v=SeH3up321Hc

- Truth for Teachers podcast: "10 Things Every White Teacher Should Know When Talking about Race in the Classroom" episode
  https://truthforteachers.com/truth-for-teachers-podcast/10-things-every-White-teacher-know-talking-race

- Teaching While White podcast
  https://www.teachingwhileWhite.org/podcast

- Code Switch podcast
  https://www.npr.org/podcasts/510312/codeswitch

- Teaching Hard History podcast
  https://www.learningforjustice.org/podcasts

- Yo, Is This Racist? podcast
  https://podcasts.apple.com/us/podcast/yo-is-this-racist/id566985372

Videos to Learn about Race and History

These resources are for teachers, not for elementary students.

Lesser-Known Facts: Slavery

- "Ex-slaves Talk About Slavery in the USA"
  https://www.youtube.com/watch?v=fZfcc21c6Uo

- "Inside the Discovery of the Last Known Slave Ship"
  youtube.com/watch?v=b1niYRK1WYI

- "Human Zoos: America's Forgotten History of Scientific Racism"
  https://www.youtube.com/watch?v=nY6Zrol5QEk

- "Were There Slaves in Alabama in the 1950s?"
  https://www.youtube.com/watch?v=nQCmQaHL5Yw

- "Genealogist Who Tracks Down Modern-Day Slavery Practices"
  https://www.youtube.com/watch?v=6OXbJHsKB3I

Racial Wealth Gap

- Explained | Racial Wealth Gap
  https://www.youtube.com/watch?v=Mqrhn8khGLM

- "Income Inequality Affects Minorities, Less Educated in Post-Pandemic Recovery"
  https://www.youtube.com/watch?v=tviGy8irNUM

- "Hearing: Examining the Racial Wealth Gap in the US"
  https://www.youtube.com/watch?v=ylVSSPtD-GOM&t=3357s

- "How Corporate America Is Failing Black Employees"
  https://www.youtube.com/watch?v=BNac_P5755Y

- "How Income Inequality Became a Big Issue Among Asian Americans"
  https://www.youtube.com/watch?v=_61OK651AsQ

Breaking Up of Minority Families

- "The War on Drugs Is Designed to Discriminate"
  https://www.youtube.com/watch?v=Xf5qFIpJ2sk

- "Systemic Racism Embedded in Foster Care to Prison Pipeline"
  https://www.youtube.com/watch?v=rxpxhmJyJys

- "How the US Stole Thousands of Native American Children"
  https://www.youtube.com/watch?v=UGqWRyBCHhw

- "Schools Tried to Forcibly Assimilate Indigenous Kids. Can the US Make Amends?"
  https://www.youtube.com/watch?v=gRNcCCgnauI

- "Native American Boarding Schools"
  https://www.youtube.com/watch?v=Yo1bYj-R7Fo

Black Employment Rates and Small Businesses

- "Freakonomics—What's in a Name?"
  https://econ.video/2019/10/31/freakonomics

- "Black Americans in the Workplace"
  https://www.youtube.com/watch?v=wALwzjVwM7g

- "Why Black-Owned Businesses Don't Survive"
  https://www.youtube.com/watch?v=MV4Nq1GaIAA

Burning of Minority Cities

- "US City Apologises for Destroying Chinatown in 1887 Arson Attack"
  https://www.youtube.com/watch?v=oyLfjpt9Mpc

- "The Largest Lynching in US History"
  https://www.youtube.com/watch?v=UpZZf7K12pU

- "The Massacre of Tulsa's 'Black Wall Street'"
  https://www.youtube.com/watch?v=x-ItsPBTFO0

- "LA Burning: The Riots 25 Years Later—Gun Store Manager David Joo Looks Back"
  https://www.youtube.com/watch?v=OCYT9Hew9ZU

Redlining, Gentrification, and the Impact Today

- "Housing Segregation and Redlining in America: A Short History"
  https://www.youtube.com/watch?v=O5FBJyqfoLM

- "Racial Segregation and Concentrated Poverty: The History of Housing in Black America"
  https://www.youtube.com/watch?v=Mi9sjhISYfg

- "How Redlining Shaped Black America as We Know It"
  https://www.youtube.com/watch?v=2o-yDowGxAc

- "Priced Out: Portland's History of Segregation and Redlining"
  https://www.youtube.com/watch?v=vMZYiv_jf2U

- "Why Are Schools Still So Segregated?"
  https://www.youtube.com/watch?v=v2TG9n0vc-4

Restrictive Voter Laws

- "How Restrictive Voting Requirements Target Minorities"
  https://www.youtube.com/watch?v=BO5uTxeY7xc

- "Voter Restriction Laws: Why Republican States Are Changing Them"
  https://www.youtube.com/watch?v=FCK4tFsNw3Q

- "The History of Black Voter Suppression—And the Fight for the Right to Vote"
  https://www.youtube.com/watch?v=-DKLM18zc5g

- "The First Chinese American Woman to Vote in the US"
  https://www.youtube.com/watch?v=viCq9LfKVwU

Latinos and Civil Rights

- "Civil Rights and Hispanics in Texas"
  https://www.youtube.com/watch?v=dzfdINufpSE

- "Cesar Chavez: American Civil Rights Activist—Fast Facts"
  https://www.youtube.com/watch?v=Wznw9TA2jXk

- "The Chicano Moratorium: Why 30,000 People Marched Through East LA in 1970"
  https://www.youtube.com/watch?v=bpj9Man7L1U

Asian Americans and World War II

- "Diary Reveals Reality of Living in a WWII Japanese Internment Camp"
  https://www.youtube.com/watch?v=xEXW153g2wI

- "Ugly History: Japanese American Incarceration Camps"
  https://www.youtube.com/watch?v=hI4N0VWq87M

- "Asian Americans Have Always Fought for Their Place in the US"
  https://www.youtube.com/watch?v=zZxFLvNLyOY

History of Immigration

- "The Racist History of US Immigration Policy"
  https://www.youtube.com/watch?v=6yiQAmgI5s4

- "What Was the Impact of the Chinese Exclusion Act?"
  https://www.youtube.com/watch?v=FbBatK7JWYc

- "Angel Island–A Story of Chinese Immigration"
  https://www.youtube.com/watch?v=OMVzI4xpPp4

- "100 Years of Immigration to the US, 1919 to 2019"
  youtube.com/watch?v=GlJg2h2NrTM

Indigenous Genocide Theft of Land

- "How the Brutal Trail of Tears Got Its Name"
  https://www.youtube.com/watch?v=SosZ2ZRJymU

- "The "Indian Problem""
  https://www.youtube.com/watch?v=if-BOZgWZPE

- "The First Thanksgiving: What Really Happened"
  https://www.youtube.com/watch?v=ociHVDWxDaY

Kingdom of Hawaii

- "Queen Liliʻuokalani–The First and Last Queen of Hawaiʻi"
  https://www.youtube.com/watch?v=gH5TJ5JTTFw

- "History Summarized: Hawaiʻi"
  https://www.youtube.com/watch?v=xYouQESFE2A

- "Hawaiian King Kalaniʻōpuʻu Meets Captain Cook–Drunk History"
  https://www.youtube.com/watch?v=agsiFcRGAQo

- "Captain Cook Was a Murderer"
  https://www.youtube.com/watch?v=qL52K_YlViY

- "The Amazing Life and Strange Death of Captain Cook: Crash Course World History #27"
  https://www.youtube.com/watch?v=2yXNrLTddME

Alaska

- "Alaska Native People and Activities, circa 1940s"
  https://www.youtube.com/watch?v=v7AFaWmrgLU

- "See How Unangax̂ Culture and Dance Resurrected, Despite WWII Internment Camps"
  https://www.youtube.com/watch?v=C4I9aOxLAUo

- "The Modern History of Alaska (1741-1959)"
  https://www.youtube.com/watch?v=eygdIcrktPU

Videos about Current Events

- "Black Lives Matter Explained: The History of a Movement"
  https://www.youtube.com/watch?v=YG8GjlLbbvs

- "Black Lives Matter Protests around World"
  https://www.youtube.com/watch?v=4Vl4IoweXPU

- "Voices from the Black Lives Matter Protests (A Short Film)"
  https://www.youtube.com/watch?v=gS2MG2k9BlM

Native Fight for Land

- "This Is the Story of Alaska Natives' Fight for Their Land"
  https://www.youtube.com/watch?v=50_kse-Uh-g

- "Alaskan Native Elders Tell Their Climate Change Story: After the Ice"
  https://www.youtube.com/watch?v=OzMkyeYP7NM

- "Mexican Americans Are Still fighting for Land They Were Promised Generations Ago"
  https://www.youtube.com/watch?v=DfkrrcrMvIo

- "Why Native Americans Are Buying Back Land That Was Stolen from Them"
  https://www.youtube.com/watch?v=kjSNL40GDO8

- "What Really Happened at Standing Rock: I Was There"
  https://www.youtube.com/watch?v=J1yD2J8vHAk

- *Standing Above the Clouds*—PBS documentary

American Indian Misconceptions and Culture

- "6 Misconceptions About Native American People"
  https://www.youtube.com/watch?v=GHdW_LVfn28

- "What People Get Wrong About Alaska Natives"
  https://www.youtube.com/watch?v=lDU4PkSqWsQ

- *Gather*—Netflix documentary

Missing and Murdered Indigenous People

- "How Prejudice Affects Official Search for Missing Indigenous Women, Other Women of Color"
  https://www.youtube.com/watch?v=VniwyAqemlo

- "Indigenous Women Keep Going Missing in Montana"
  https://www.youtube.com/watch?v=iboGDAPeymo

- "The Search: Missing and Murdered Indigenous Women"
  https://www.youtube.com/watch?v=mdPvoNDfMbA&t=156s

Children of Color in Foster Care

- "Who Should Be Allowed to Adopt Native American Children?"
  https://www.youtube.com/watch?v=hi7fOOCbI-8

- "Unpacking How Child Welfare and Foster Care Fail Black Children"
  https://www.youtube.com/watch?v=9u689ytgWLY

Anti-Asian Hate

- "The History of Anti-Asian Hate Crimes in America"
  https://www.youtube.com/watch?v=JX-GD4fGFHk

- "Asian Americans Speak Out: Countering the Rise in Anti-Asian Hate"
  https://www.youtube.com/watch?v=OkWrZoK7Wro

- "We Need to Talk About Anti-Asian Hate"
  https://www.youtube.com/watch?v=14WUuya94QE

Latino Identity and Representation

- "Hispanic Americans Reflect on Immigration, Culture, and Identity"
  https://www.youtube.com/watch?v=H2UThoqyZuQ

- "Why Aren't DC and Puerto Rico States? It's Complicated"
  https://www.youtube.com/watch?v=21AybYIoVNs

- "Actor Edward James Olmos Fights to Get More Latino Representation in Hollywood"
  https://www.youtube.com/watch?v=QZjfHjYVpRE

Primary Source Photos

These are listed in no particular order.

- Slavery Images: A Visual Record of the African Slave Trade and Slave Life in the Early African Diaspora
  http://slaveryimages.org

- Library of Congress has a map collection
  https://www.loc.gov/maps/collections

- Edward S. Curtis's The North American Indian
  http://curtis.library.northwestern.edu

- The New York Public Library Digital Collections
  https://digitalcollections.nypl.org

- Buffalo Bill Center of the West Digital Collections for Plains Indians
  https://centerofthewest.org/research/mccracken-research-library/digital-collections/plains-indians

- University of Washington African American History collection
  https://guides.lib.uw.edu/c.php?g=344236&p=2319730

- South Asian American Digital Archive
  https://www.saada.org

- University of California Japanese American Relocation Digital Archive
  https://calisphere.org/exhibitions/t11/jarda

- Yale University Library Latinx Studies: Digital Primary Sources
  https://guides.library.yale.edu/c.php?g=512493&p=3511584

- University of Southern California Digital Libraries
  https://digitallibrary.usc.edu

- Seminar on the Acquisition of Latin American Library Materials
  https://salalm.org

CLOSING THOUGHTS

It's a lot. Change is never easy, especially when it is something as sensitive as dealing with race and examining your own biases. I hope I have made it a little easier to access resources to do this. It'll never be easy or comfortable to confront your own opportunities for improvement.

Do not rush yourself. Take time to absorb the information and reflect. Set this book down and come back to it. I have had to do this in writing. Some of the information is hard to stomach. Self-care is important.

I hope I have encouraged you to add something new to your classroom or to take the time to listen to a podcast. You are shaping the minds of children every year. You can give them a strong foundation to move forward in their school career. You can arm them with knowledge and tools to examine the world around them.

You may not be able to change legislation or policy. You may not be able to change your school's procedures, but you can change the perspective of a classroom of students. You can support the students at a disadvantage and let them know you see them.

GLOSSARY

BIPOC—Black, Indigenous, People of Color

Code switching—Alternating between two languages or customs depending on the audience.

Colonization—The destruction of native populations and customs in order for European and Western powers to benefit politically or economically.

Colorism—A stereotype based on the lightness or darkness of people's skin.

DACA—Deferred Action for Childhood Arrivals is a US immigration policy that defers the deportation of children who entered the country unlawfully.

Dog whistle—An example of a microaggression used in a way in which people outside of the target race may not pick up on the significance.

DREAM—The Development, Relief, and Education for Alien Minors Act grants temporary residency with the right to work to undocumented immigrants who entered the US as children; children who qualify for the DREAM Act are known as Dreamers.

Equality—Every student is given the same resources in order to succeed.

Equity—Students are given specialized tools based on their needs.

Implicit bias—An attitude or belief about certain people or groups that someone holds without realizing it.

Microaggressions—Discrimination that is subtle, indirect, and sometimes unintentional.

Model minority myth—A misconception that falsely elevates Asian Americans above other races to ignore oppression and pit races against each other.

Native Science—An understanding of the environment or natural world through indigenous traditions.

Poverty trap—A cycle that makes it difficult for impoverished people to escape being poor.

Unauthorized or undocumented immigrant—An immigrant who enters the US without proper paperwork or who has overstayed a visas.

REFERENCES

"An Introduction to South Asian American History." South Asian American Digital Archive (SAADA). July 30, 2015. https://www.saada.org/resources/introduction.

"Alaska Native Experiences." National Park Service. Last updated August 5, 2021. https://www.nps.gov/aleu/learn/historyculture/unangax-aleut-experiences.htm.

Asante-Muhammad, Dedrick "Challenges to Native American Advancement: The Recession and Native America." *Dedrick Asante-Muhammad* (blog). November 18, 2019. https://bridgingtheracialwealthdivide.wordpress.com/2019/11/18/challenges-to-native-american-advancement-the-recession-and-native-america.

Asante-Muhammad, Dedrick, and Kathy Ramirez. "The Economic Reality of Native Americans and the Need for Immediate Repair." NCRC.org. November 26, 2019. https://ncrc.org/the-economic-reality-of-native-americans-and-the-need-for-immediate-repair.

Bajaj, Monisha, Ameena Ghaffar-Kucher, and Karishma Desai. "Brown Bodies and Xenophobic Bullying in US Schools: Critical Analysis and Strategies for Action." *Harvard Educational Review* 86, no. 4 (2016): 481–505. https://doi.org/10.17763/1943-5045-86.4.481.

Bajaj, Monisha, Ameena Ghaffar-Kucher, and Karishma Desai. "In the Face of Xenophobia: Lessons to Aaddress Bbullying of South Asian American Youth." South Asian Americans Leading Togetherg (SAALT). 2013. https://saalt.org/wp-content/uploads/2012/09/In-the-Face-of-Xenophobia.pdf.

Barlow, Jameta N. "Black Women, the Forgotten Survivors of Sexual Assault." American Psychological Association. 2020. https://www.apa.org/pi/about/newsletter/2020/02/black-women-sexual-assault.

"Black Women Aren't Paid Fairly, and That Hits Harder in an Economic Crisis." Lean In. https://leanin.org/data-about-the-gender-pay-gap-for-black-women.

"Block the Vote: How Politicians Are Trying to Block Voters from the Ballot Box." ACLU.org. Last updated August 18, 2021. https://www.aclu.org/news/civil-liberties/block-the-vote-voter-suppression-in-2020.

Broderick, Francis and Michael Burwell. *Aleutian Voices: Forced to Leave: The Evacuation of Unangax from the Aleutians During World War II.* Volume 2, No. 1. Washington, D.C.: Park Service, 2015.

Budiman, Abby and Neil G. Ruiz. "Key Facts about Asian Americans, a Diverse and Growing Population." Pew Research Center. April 9, 2021. https://www.pewresearch.org/fact-tank/2021/04/29/key-facts-about-asian-americans.

Collins, Chuck, Darrick Hamilton, Dedrick Asante-Muhammed, and Josh Hoxie. "Ten Solutions to Bridge the Racial Wealth Divide." Institute for Policy Studies. April 2019. https://ips-dc.org/report-racial-wealth-divide-solutions.

Contreras, Russell. "Biden Orders New Initiative to Probe Challenges around Latino Education as Population Grows." Axios. September 13, 2021. https://www.axios.com/biden-new-initiative-hispanic-education-college-c51352c6-1b08-4dc4-9c6d-654d73397dac.html.

Fairlie, Robert W., and Alicia M. Robb. "Disparities in Capital Access between Minority and Non-minority-Owned Businesses: The Troubling Reality of Capital Limitations Faced by MBEs." US Department of Commerce, Minority Business Development Agency. 2010. https://archive.mbda.gov/page/executive-summary-disparities-capital-access-between-minority-and-non-minority-businesses.html.

"Fast Facts: Degrees Conferred by Race and Sex." National Center for Educational Statistics. 2019. https://nces.ed.gov/fastfacts/display.asp?id=72.

Fisher, Max. "16 Maps That Americans Don't Like to Talk About." Vox. May 27, 2015. https://www.vox.com/2015/5/27/8618261/america-maps-truths.

"Four Seasons." Crayola.com. https://www.crayola.com/lesson-plans/four-seasons-lesson-plan.

"Incidents and Offenses." FBI.gov. October 29, 2019. https://ucr.fbi.gov/hate-crime/2019/topic-pages/incidents-and-offenses.

Kendi, Ibram X., *How to Be an Antiracist.* London: Vintage, 2021.

Kleinrock, Liz. "How to Teach Kids to Talk about Taboo Topics," TED Talk, February 20, 2019. https://ed.ted.com/lessons/how-to-teach-kids-to-talk-about-taboo-topics-liz-kleinrock.

Kline, Patrick M., Evan K. Rose, and Christopher R. Walters. "Systemic Discrimination among Large US Employers." National Bureau of Economic Research. 2021. doi.org/ 10.3386/w29053.

Kochhar, Rakesh, and Anthony Cilluffo. "Income Inequality in the US Is Rising Most Rapidly among Asians." Pew Research Center. July 12, 2018. https://www.pewresearch.org/social-trends/2018/07/12/income-inequality-in-the-u-s-is-rising-most-rapidly-among-asians.

Krogstad, Jens Manuel. "5 Facts about Latinos and Education." Pew Research Center. July 18, 2016. https://www.pewresearch.org/fact-tank/2016/07/28/5-facts-about-latinos-and-education.

"Learning in Ohio." Ohio Department of Education. https://education.ohio .gov/Topics/Learning-in-Ohio.

Leman, Jennifer. "7 Indigenous Pioneers You Need to Know." *Popular Mechanics*. October 14, 2019. https://www.popularmechanics.com /science/g29460020/indigenous-scientists.

Lubbers, Payne. "Job Applicants with 'Black Names' Still Less Likely to Get Interviews." Bloomberg. July 29, 2021. https://www.bloomberg.com /news/articles/2021-07-29/job-applicants-with-black-names-still-less -likely-to-get-the-interview.

Milner IV, Richard H., and Kofi Lomotey. *Handbook of Urban Education*. London: Routledge, 2013.

"Murdered and Missing Indigenous Women." National Women's Wilderness. https://www.nativewomenswilderness.org/mmiw.

Moore, Eddie, Ali Michael, Marguerite W. Penick-Parks, Glenn E. Singleton, and Heather Hackman. *The Guide for White Women Who Teach Black Boys: Understanding, Connecting, Respecting*. Thousand Oaks, CA. Corwin, 2018.

Morrison, Aaron. "50-Year War on Drugs Imprisoned Millions of Black Americans." Associated Press. July 23, 2021. https://apnews.com/article /war-on-drugs-75e61c224de3a394235df80de7d70b70.

"NĀ Hopena Aʻo (HĀ)." OHE Hub. Accessed December 5, 2021. https:// sites.google.com/k12.hi.us/ohehub/n%C4%81-hopena-a%CA%BBo -h%C4%81.

"Negative Effects of Positive Stereotypes." Stereotypes, Identity, and Belonging Lab. University of Washington. Accessed December 4, 2021. https://depts.washington.edu/sibl/negative-effects-of-positive -stereotypes.

Nichols, Hedreich, Leigh Ann Erickson, and Wing Kelisa. *Racial Justice in America: Topics for Change*. Ann Arbor, MI: Sleeping Bear Press, 2021.

ParentCo. "The Best Age for Kids to Learn a Second Language." *ParentCo*. July 26, 2021. https://www.parent.com/blogs/conversations/the-best -age-for-kids-to-learn-a-second-language.

Passel, Jeffrey S., and D'Vera Cohn. "U.S. Unauthorized Immigrants Are More Proficient in English, More Educated Than a Decade Ago." Pew Research Center. May 23, 2019. https://www.pewresearch.org /fact-tank/2019/05/23/u-s-undocumented-immigrants-are-more -proficient-in-english-more-educated-than-a-decade-ago.

Regan, Sheila. "'It's Cultural Genocide:' Inside the Fight to Stop a Pipeline on Tribal Lands." *The Guardian*. February 19, 2021. https://www .theguardian.com/us-news/2021/feb/19/line-3-pipeline-ojibwe-tribal -lands.

Rodríguez, Noreen N. "Focus on Friendship or Fights for Civil Rights? Teaching the Difficult History of Japanese American Incarceration

through the Bracelet." *Occasional Paper Series*, no. 44 (2020). https://
educate.bankstreet.edu/occasional-paper-series/vol2020/iss44/6.

Silverman, David J. "In 1621, the Wampanoag Tribe Had Its Own Agenda."
The Atlantic. November 27, 2019. https://www.theatlantic.com/ideas
/archive/2019/11/thanksgiving-belongs-wampanoag-tribe/602422.

Spocchia, Gina. "145 Years After White Residents Burned Down a
California Chinatown, the City Apologizes." *Independent UK*. July 30,
2021. https://www.independent.co.uk/news/world/americas/chinatown
-california-apology-antioch-asian-b1893865.html.

Solano, Francisco. "Photoprotection and Skin Pigmentation: Melanin-Related
Molecules and Some Other New Agents Obtained from Natural Sources."
Molecules 25, no. 7 (2020): 1537. doi.org/10.3390/molecules25071537.

"State Standards and Frameworks in Social Studies." Maryland State
Department of Education. https://marylandpublicschools.org/about
/Pages/DCAA/Social-Studies/MSSS.aspx.

Stechyson, Natalie. "Kids Books Still Have a Lack-of-Diversity Problem,
Powerful Image Shows." Huffington Post. Last updated July 3,. 2019.
https://www.huffpost.com/entry/diversity-kids-books-statistics_l_610875
01e4b0497e67026f1c.

Suitts, Steve. *Overturning Brown: The Segregationist Legacy of the Modern
School Choice Movement*. Montgomery, AL: NewSouth Books, 2020.

USC Dornsife College of Letters, Arts, and Sciences. "*In Conversation with
Viet Thanh Nguyen*." YouTube Video, 1:01:07. April 13, 2021. https://
www.youtube.com/watch?v=lTsX3i2IwEU.

Vickery, Amanda Elizabeth, and Noreen Naseem Rodríguez. "'A Woman
Question and a Race Problem': Attending to Intersectionality in
Children's Literature." *The Social Studies* 112, no. 2 (2020): 57–62. https://
doi.org/10.1080/00377996.2020.1809979.

Weitz, Jared. "Why Minorities Have So Much Trouble Accessing Small
Business Loans." *Forbes*. January 22, 2018. https://www.forbes.com
/sites/forbesfinancecouncil/2018/01/22/why-minorities-have-so-much
-trouble-accessing-small-business-loans/?sh=4dad5b1355c4.

Wing Sue, Derald, Christina M. Capodilupo, Gina C. Torino, Jennifer M.
Bucceri, Aisha M. B. Holder, Kevin L. Nadal, and Marta Esquilin. "Racial
Microaggressions in Everyday Life: Implications for Clinical Practice."
The *American Psychologist* 62, no. 4 (2007): 271–86. doi.org/10.1037
/0003-066X.62.4.271.

"Who Is Most Affected by the School to Prison Pipeline?" School of
Education. February 24, 2021. https://soeonline.american.edu/blog
/school-to-prison-pipeline.

Work Projects Administration. *Slave Narratives: A Folk History of
Slavery in the US, From Interviews with Former Slaves*. Charleston, SC:
BiblioBazaar, 2007.

ACKNOWLEDGMENTS

This book would not have been possible without educators like you who wish to make their classrooms a better, more equitable place. Making changes and confronting implicit biases within yourself are challenging and uncomfortable. It's exhausting and tiresome. Thank you for taking the time to purchase and read this material.

Thank you to my editors for their diligent work and desire to make the classrooms a better place. Thank you to the illustrators for bringing the vision to life. Thank you to Ulysses Press for putting the information on shelves and in the hands of teachers.

Thank you to my past students, who shaped my career and will continue to shape the lives of their teachers. Thank you to everyone who has taken the time to speak with me on these issues. Your work and knowledge have been invaluable. Even if it only helps one teacher, that one teacher is responsible for almost 30 minds every year.

Thank you to my therapist and my family who have listened to me rant about injustice and the history of racism. You have helped me carry the weight and burden of knowledge. As you know, I am not one for many soft words.

ABOUT THE AUTHOR

Aja Hannah has worked with preschool and elementary school children in Maryland, Pennsylvania, Colorado, Ohio, and Hawaii since the early 2000s. In her work throughout the US, she saw opportunities for racial equity in the classroom and a desire from the students to learn.

In 2011, she graduated with honors with a bachelor of arts degree in English and journalism. With eight years' experience as a writer and editor, Hannah has written for national and international publications, including *The Independent, The Progressive,* and *Destination Cleveland.*

She lives with her two young children and splits her time between Washington, DC, and Ohio.